D0251107

THE VINE LIFE

Other books by Colleen Townsend Evans:

A New Joy
Love Is an Everyday Thing
Start Loving: The Miracle of Forgiving
My Lover, My Friend (with Louis Evans)
Teaching Your Child to Pray

THE VINE LIFE

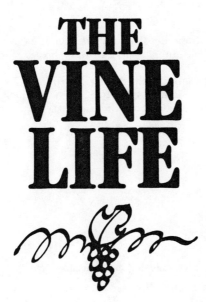

Colleen Townsend Evans

Published by
√chosen books
Lincoln, Virginia 22078
Distributed by Word Books • Waco, Texas 76703

Unless otherwise indicated, all Scripture quotations are taken from the Revised Standard Version of the Bible, copyright 1946, 1952, © 1971, 1973. Used by permission.

Scripture quotations identified as TLB are from *The Living Bible*, copyright 1971 by Tyndale House Publishers, Wheaton, Ill. Used by permission.

Scripture quotations identified TEV are from the *Good News Bible*—New Testament: Copyright © American Bible Society 1966, 1971, 1976.

Scripture quotations identified PHILLIPS are from *The New Testament in Modern English* (Revised Edition), © J. B. Phillips 1958, 1960, 1972. Used by permission of Macmillan Publishing Co., Inc.

Library of Congress Cataloging in Publication Data

Evans, Colleen Townsend.
   The vine life.

   1. Christian life—Presbyterian authors.   2. Bible.
N.T.   John XV—Criticism, interpretation, etc.
3. Evans, Colleen Townsend.   I. Title.
BV4501.2.E873   248.4′851   79-25646

ISBN 0-912376-40-6

To

The covenant brothers and sisters—
partners in abiding.

Acknowledgments

People I want to thank—

Those who choose to be nameless who have shared their stories—and their ideas.

Robert Pratt, special assistant in environment, Department of Food and Agriculture for the State of California, who provided ideas and information on vines and general viticulture.

My husband's secretary—and my special friend—Marjorie Cook, who took time after hours to do some last-minute typing for me. Thanks, Cookie!

And most especially my gratitude to three of my sisters in the Lord whose help was invaluable. I'm certain this project could not have reached fruition—not this year, anyway—without their gifts—

Margaret Gray Towne, my biologist friend who supplied much of the botanical material throughout the book as well as sharing her sensitive spiritual insights with me, and

Irene Burk Harrell, an editor and writer in her own right, who took my sheafs of material ("Enough for two books—stop!") and made order out of chaos, and

Linda LeSourd, long a treasured friend—and increasingly, a partner in ministry.

Last, but by no means least, my thanks to Leonard LeSourd, wonderful friend and editor extraordinary at Chosen Books.

Table of Contents

The heart of the matter is that we are to trust God, not ourselves. Our strength and might are perfectly irrelevant in God's plan. We can do nothing on our own and God intends for us to learn that.

JOHN ALEXANDER
From *The Other Side*

The Scripture

John 15 (RSV)

I am the true Vine, and My Father is the Vinedresser. Every branch of Mine that bears no fruit, He takes away, and every branch that does bear fruit He prunes, that it may bear more fruit. You are already made clean by the word which I have spoken to you. Abide in Me, and I in you. As the branch cannot bear fruit by itself, unless it abides in the vine, neither can you, unless you abide in Me. I am the Vine, you are the branches. He who abides in Me, and I in him, he it is that bears much fruit, for apart from Me you can do nothing. If a man does not abide in Me, he is cast forth as a branch and withers; and the branches are gathered, thrown into the fire and burned. If you abide in Me, and My words abide in you, ask whatever you will, and it shall be done for you. By this My Father is glorified, that you bear much fruit, and so prove to be My disciples. As the Father has loved Me, so have I loved you; abide in My love. If you keep My commandments, you will abide in My love, just as I have kept My Father's commandments and abide in His love. These things I have spoken to you, that My joy may be in you, and that your joy may be full.

This is My commandment, that you love one another as I have loved you. Greater love has no man than this, that a man lay down his life for his friends . . .

If the world hates you, know that it has hated Me before it hated you. If you were of the world, the world would love its own; but because you are not of the world, but I chose you out of the world, therefore the world hates you . . . If they persecuted Me, they will persecute you . . . But when the Counselor comes, whom I shall send you from the Father, even the Spirit of truth, who proceeds from the Father, He will bear witness to Me.

How It All Began

When I was very small our country was caught in the grip of the Great Depression. Life was hard, and to simplify our situation my mother and I moved in with my grandfather. Poverty was widespread and I can remember, even as a child, the hurt inside me when I heard that other people literally were starving to death. At least we had food on the table. Yet something tugged at me to try and help these people who were hungry.

In the backyard I had a playhouse that my other grandfather had built for me. The furnishings included a small but real electric stove, with little coil burners that got warm enough to heat cocoa or soup.

One morning while playing in my little house, I happened to look out the window as Mother put a newspaper-wrapped bundle into the garbage can by the back door of the big house. It was the week after Thanksgiving, and I thought the bundle might have at least one discarded turkey bone in it. Bones were good for making soup, I remembered. Hadn't I seen my mother use them many times? She was a genius at making things stretch, and in those days no one could afford to waste anything.

After Mother had returned to the house, I went to the garbage can and lifted the lid. Gingerly unfolding the soggy newspaper bundle, I made a wonderful discovery. There was not just one turkey bone but a whole pile of them in the midst of some clean-looking potato peelings and a handful of still-warm coffee grounds. I ran back to my playhouse and grabbed my biggest pan from the tiny cupboard. Crouching beside an outside water faucet, I washed the coffee grounds off the bones and filled the pot with water. While it began to heat on the stove, I sprinkled salt and pepper until the little shakers were nearly empty. Then I tasted the soup. Pretty good. *But some vegetables would make it even better*, I thought. Surely nobody would care if I got a stalk of celery and a carrot or two and maybe an onion from grandfather's kitchen.

When the vegetables had been added, a friend came to play. She agreed to go about the neighborhood and round up starving children—children I knew had to be out there just waiting for my invitation. I was disappointed when only three or four came back with her; they were just neighborhood kids like me, not starving urchins at all. Nevertheless, they lined up outside my window and took the little painted tin teacups of soup which I solemnly handed out, all the while feeling like the mother of the whole world.

"When I grow up," I told myself, "I'll work in a soup kitchen—or be a helper in an orphanage. No, I'll have my own orphanage. I'll have a job where I can help other people all the time."

During the summer between my high school and college years, I worked in the orphanage of the California Children's Home Society. Getting up at four in the morning in order to be at work at five was a challenge since I had never been a bright-eyed "morning person." Nevertheless, I hung in there, and in my crisply starched and ironed nursery uniform I bathed the infants and gave them their first bottles of the day.

The work was satisfying, the babies were comforted, and I felt good about it. But I kept yearning to make a real difference in the lives of people. In the aftermath of World War II that yearning prompted me to join a group of young volunteers who traveled overseas to help rebuild some of the most devastated, war-torn areas of Europe.

One summer we built a barracks outside Paris for refugees. The next summer I joined a hundred young people from all over the world, and together we built a road to a religious conference center high in the Italian Alps. What a satisfying experience it was to work on a project in which we all believed.

I was a "doer," no doubt about it, seeking after a nameless satisfaction. My search usually took the form of working harder, trying to do more, for that was the emphasis in the church in which I grew up. It was only natural that I wanted to pursue a career in social work for this seemed to be the best way to help people.

During my student years I worked as a model to help pay my college expenses. This led to a successful screen test and a contract with a movie studio. It was hardly the social service career I had envisioned for myself, but it would help me finance my education. Since acting called for a lot of extra homework, soon I was going to plays and visiting theaters, eager to learn all there was to know about my new profession. One night after attending a local college performance with a date, we went backstage. In the wings, I saw someone who looked familiar. As he gave me a quizzical glance, I asked, "Say, aren't you Louie Evans?"

He smiled, "And aren't you Coke Townsend?" He used the nickname that had stuck with me all through school. He had been at the performance that night—which was given at the college he attended—and had gone backstage, as had I, to greet the cast.

Although we had attended high school together, we had not seen one another since then. However, after this brief reunion we began dating on a casual basis.

One night he called me with a note of excitement in his voice and asked to see me. His tone was so serious, curiosity overwhelmed me.

When he showed up at the front door, I could *see* a difference, too. He simply glowed! As we drove down Sunset Strip I studied his profile and noted how strong it was. He told me he had just returned from Forest Home, a Christian conference center in the San Bernardino mountains. The speaker of the week was Dr. Henrietta Mears, the dynamic director of Christian education at Hollywood Presbyterian Church, where Louie's father was pastor. We turned into a drive-in where he ordered hamburgers and milkshakes for both of us.

As we ate, Louie told me what had happened. At the Monday night meeting Dr. Mears' message had stimulated him to consider the tremendous need for leadership in the world. Louie and several others sought out Dr. Mears after the meeting. As they prayed together the Holy Spirit came upon each of them in a different way. For Louie, it was shattering as he saw his self-sufficiency and pride through God's eyes and was broken with humiliating insight. Sensing this was the time to give over the "whole mess," he yielded a proud will and surrendered it all to Christ.

"Christ became a reality to me at that moment, Coke. I'll never be the same again."

Louie was elated as if he had told me the most wonderful secret in all the world. I just sat there, baffled, not knowing what to say.

In the weeks that followed, Louie introduced me to the friends who had shared this life-changing experience with him. All of them were radiantly turned on about something. And the word that was on their lips more than any other was not "church" or "religion" but "Jesus." It was as if they knew Him personally.

I found myself puzzled as they shared their stories, because I had the feeling they fully expected me to want the same experience they had found. But I didn't see that I needed it.

Months later Louie talked me into attending a retreat, again at Forest Home. It was delightful being in the mountains I loved, but even more wonderful was the impact of two days of listening to people of great diversity tell about a common relationship—new and real—they had found with a living Lord. Finally my ears (or was it my heart?) were opened to what they were saying. I saw suddenly that it was not religion they were talking about; it was not works; it was not ethics or morality; neither was it going to church or doing any number of things I'd done already. Their exhilarating secret—so hard for my mind to grasp—wasn't a matter of doing anything. It wasn't trying harder. The secret was surrender: giving one's self to a vital relationship with Jesus Christ, who was doing for them and through them what they could never do for themselves.

Wasn't that what I was really looking for? I was already a believer in God, but did I also need to surrender to Jesus Christ? Did I need to let Him take over and live His life in me? The questions raced through my head during the meetings.

But how, Lord? How can You live Your life in me?

Later, when I couldn't sleep, I tiptoed outside for a quiet walk. I sat on a rock alongside a tree on the conference grounds and without emotion I said: "All right, God. You know I believe in You. And if the reason I don't have the completeness I've been seeking is that I've never really surrendered to Your Son Jesus, then that's what I'd like to do right now."

It was so simple—an almost matter-of-fact capitulation,

and a resulting quiet joy as I felt wrapped in a blanket of love. Somehow by that act of surrendering, I had found the object of my searching. He was a Person, a real Person!

When I crept back to my bunk in the little cabin, I sensed my life would never be the same again. After that new beginning, Louie and I began spending more time together. We became great friends, and our friendship then became the basis for falling in love—and marriage a few years later.

The two decades plus between then and now have been times of growing and stretching—rearing four children who have been a source of deep satisfaction—experiencing as a family the agony and sheer joy of being committed to and loving one another until it hurts.

Always, Christ has been the central focus of our life together. And yet this question of how to let Jesus live His life in us has not been simply, or quickly, or completely resolved.

Not long ago, Louie and I went to a dinner party with a dozen old friends, all in middle life, who hadn't seen one another in years. Some were pastors of churches; others were involved with Young Life, Faith at Work, and various fellowship and prayer ministries that God is using. Looking around the table I thought, *What an amazing variety of good things these people are doing for God. They really have it made.*

But as the conversation continued that night, each person bringing the others up to date on what had been happening in his or her life, everyone expressed the same longing: I don't have it made. *I need to get back to the basics* of an abiding, surrendered, dependent relationship with God.

As one man expressed it, "For years I've thought I didn't have to have a prayer time or a quiet season every day when I would just listen to God. I thought that was too legalistic for me. But I want to tell you, friends, I've come back to this practice."

I saw others nodding their heads in agreement around
the table. "Back to the Vine," someone murmured. "Abiding in the Vine in order to bear His fruit."

None of us had left God, or detoured to do his or her
own thing, but all were increasingly aware of our need
to be totally dependent on Jesus if our lives were going
to count for anything lasting.

On our way home that night, as we made ready for
bed, and even as I was drifting off to sleep, the words
kept running through my mind:

Abiding in the Vine. Abiding in the Vine.

A deep desire was kindled in me to study the 15th chapter of John to learn about the relationship between the
Vine and the branches. I hungered to soak in the words
of Jesus as He told the parable and to grow in my understanding and experience of real Vine Life.

"Lord, teach me," I prayed. "I want to know more about
what You meant when You said, 'I am the Vine, and you
are the branches. Abide in Me and I in you.' Lead me,
teach me, speak to me about Vine Life. Thank You, Lord,
for I believe You'll do it."

With that simple, whispered prayer, a new search began
in my life, a search to understand more fully the meaning
of Vine Life—and how *I* could live it.

The True Vine

Several weeks after the dinner party I sat down in my rocking chair in the corner of our bedroom to begin my study of the 15th chapter of John. But before starting the notations which would become the basis for this book, I decided to treat myself to some quiet moments—rocking, musing, reminiscing.

What memories this old rocking chair held—memories not dimmed by its new garden-green, gold and white floral slipcover. Louie had bought the chair for me—our first big purchase after our seminary years—when we had moved to Bel Air, California, to start a new church. It had been a sentimental gift—something he felt would be perfect for my role as a mother, and he was right.

How elegant the chair had been when Louie brought it home, resplendent in gold brocade upholstery. The gold brocade didn't fit our modest life style, but it had suited well the mood of my spiritual life. At the time I was a

21

relatively new Christian, with a husband, and there would soon be four babies in five years. My cup wasn't simply full—it was splashing over! There was so much of life to experience—and I was brimming with eagerness and energy for it all.

Right away the chair became my "nursing chair," where I sat to nurse our babies, to rock them to sleep, to cuddle them against my breast in the awesome wonder of new life. Our children—Dan, Tim, Andie and Jamie—came along in almost breathless succession, each one prayed for and welcomed. And to be honest—as time passed with all the new duties and responsibilities of motherhood, my energy level fell well below the rim of my cup.

When our youngest graduated into the "I-can-do-it-my-self" independence of toddlerhood, my chair assumed a new role. It became my thinking and praying chair. For the new role, it needed a new look. Shabby, soiled, thread-bare, gold brocade wouldn't do, so I had a slipcover made from a white linen-like fabric, thinking the children were now too old to want to sit in my chair. I was wrong of course.

The white slipcover lasted for years through many trips to the drycleaners and was finally replaced when we moved from Bel Air south to La Jolla. There, a bright aqua cover matched our bedspread. This time I made sure the slip-cover was not white and was washable.

My chair's "aqua season" symbolized years of learning and growth—rocking a child upon my lap, sharing something very special with each one alone. As a hopeless "bookaholic," I cherished most some of the memories of hours spent with one child at a time in the company of a favorite book, reading aloud to them and later—as they grew beyond lap-sitting and slid beside me to share the ample seat of the rocker—having them read aloud to me. Sometimes we took turns reading until an especially treas-ured book was finished.

My musings ended. I now faced the realities of children grown and found myself at the threshold of another season of life—but a season in which the chair would still be the setting for deep and profound experiences. I began organizing my study materials for the journey into the Vine Life: a threadbare old Dummelow commentary, the William Barclay Daily Study Bible commentary on John, a newer Interpreter's Bible commentary I'd borrowed from one of the boys, a concordance and several translations of the Bible. There were devotional books by Andrew Murray, a man who had much to say about the Vine Life, two books by Thomas Merton and Hudson Taylor's story of his walk with the Lord.

There were pages of notes and meticulously labeled diagrams from my botanist friend, Margaret Towne. And almost hidden among the stacks of books was a flourishing green philodendron that threatened to take over when I was not careful to prune it back. Plants do grow better when you talk to them, I've discovered.

I'm a seeker, a learner—not an expert in theology, biblical interpretation or vine dressing—and therefore quick to admit my need of assistance from those better versed than I in these things. Most of all, I asked the Lord to teach me, to open my eyes to the truths He had for me in this passage.

"I am the true Vine," Jesus began.

The first thing I noticed was that Jesus dealt with the familiar—something near at hand that everybody could understand.

In the setting where Jesus told this story there were vines growing everywhere—on terraces, in manicured gardens, creeping lazily over the ground and framing the doors of humble cottages. All over Palestine, wherever one could look, there was the vine.

The vine also was a symbol familiar to Jesus' listeners. The Old Testament often pictured Israel as the vine or vineyard of God: "For the vineyard of the Lord of hosts is the house of Israel . . ." (Isaiah 5:7). "Yet I planted you a choice vine . . ." (Jeremiah 2:21).

Again and again in the Bible, the nation and the vine were linked, until the vine, quite literally, stood for the nation of Israel in the minds of Jesus' hearers. But Jesus emphasized, "I am the *true* Vine," as if to say, "The nation of Israel is not the true Vine, I am. Don't think that because you belong to Israel by birth and are a member of My chosen people, that you are automatically a branch of the Vine of God. Only a living relationship with Me can guarantee you a place in the Kingdom. Only when you are joined to Me are you joined to God."

To the Pharisees with their stifling lists of dos and don'ts these were shocking and revolutionary words. Like others of their day—and ours—they paid more attention to their religious system than to God. I had been guilty of that— of focusing so much on good works in my past that I was bogged down, tired from trying so hard. Forgive me Lord! Now I see the vine is obviously the entire, exclusive source of life for the branch. That's exactly what Jesus means to be for me! *Only when you are joined to Me are you joined to God.* It was a revelation almost too exciting to contemplate—that I was meant to live in as close, as uninterrupted, as intimate a union with Jesus as a branch lives with a vine. And it was clear that the branch didn't have to understand *how* it could be—the branch just stays connected. Was that a lesson for me, too?

Yes, and not only that, but "My Father is the Vinedresser," Jesus went on to say.

Even before a vineyard is planted, the vinedresser is at work, carefully choosing the most satisfactory site for the vines—the right side of the right hill for the maximum benefit from light, shelter, soil, weather and geography. It seems to me that God the Vinedresser has chosen *our* location, too. For Scripture says:

"From one man He created all races of mankind and made them live throughout the whole earth. He Himself fixed beforehand the exact times and the limits of the places where they would live. He did this so that they would look for Him, and perhaps find Him as they felt around for Him" (Acts 17:26–28, TEV).

This verse meant that not only did our Vinedresser decide *where* we would live but *when* and even *why.* God Himself, the perfect Vinedresser, had put me in the very circumstance in which I found myself in order that I might look for Him and find Him! That was why the members of my family were where they were too—that they might experience God *there, now.*

Lord, how can I ever complain about where I am—when I know You have put me there?

I have learned that grapevines have to have full sun to be healthy and bear good fruit. Shady places make them susceptible to mildew. Nobody had to remind me that Jesus is the light of the world in whom no darkness can stand. I remembered that passage well, and, totally caught up in the analogy, I found joy in the thought that there are no shady places in our Lord, no places for disease to grow.

Even after the perfect, sunlit site is chosen by the vinedresser, a well-tended, productive vineyard doesn't just appear. Someone has to tend it. Allowed to grow wild, without the loving care of a gardener, it is likely to be overrun with weeds, becoming a tangled skein of woody canes which produce sparse and inferior grapes. A productive vineyard on the other hand is diligently cared for by the vinedresser. It is a delight to behold—row upon row of fruit-laden vines covering the hillside in an orderly pattern.

It was obvious to me that the branches can never take on the job of vinedresser. They can't weed themselves, mulch, prune, irrigate, spray, fertilize, cultivate, graft—

the vinedresser must do *all* that. Branches will utterly fail
in their purpose if they aren't under the care of Him who
tills the soil and tends to the plant's needs.
*That's what we had all seen about ourselves at that dinner
party,* I said to myself. Each of us wanted, above all else,
to be certain that we kept in right relationship to the Vine
and properly submitted to our heavenly Vinedresser so
our lives would not be wasted. We wanted to get back
to the basics—the basic relationships of the Christian life.
Several days later I was out in our yard, kneeling alongside a bed of azaleas. I'm not much of a gardener, but as
I worked with the good-smelling earth (asking myself why
I didn't do this more often), pulling out weeds, carefully
removing broken branches, it hit me again. The azaleas
can no more pull their own weeds, remove their own broken branches or tend to watering themselves when dry,
than I can supply the needs of my life from my own resources.
Leaning back on my heels to survey what I'd done to
make the azalea bed a thing of beauty again instead of
an eyesore filled with scraggly growth, I thought of the
unkempt areas of my life—too little discipline in my prayer
time in spite of firm resolves; the still-burgeoning vitality
of the "try harder" syndrome; the frustration that welled
up when my well-planned schedule met head-on with una-
voidable interruptions day after day. I knew suddenly I
would always be helpless to mend my own situation.
Yes, I needed a heavenly Gardener, all right. How many
times I had been aware of His weeding thorny situations
from my path, of His mulching the soil of my life with
nurturing relationships, of His cultivating and encouraging positive and good influences. I knew that He had done
what was needed to keep me healthy to grow and bear
fruit for Him. And I was confident He would continue
to do it.
At that moment, Breezy, our family golden retriever,
came sniffing by, and I saw another truth about my rela-

tionship with the Vinedresser. Just yesterday I had given
Breezy a bath and treated her for fleas. She's our son Dan's
dog, really, and he usually keeps her presentable, but he
was out of town for a few days. We'd had a rain, so there
had been plenty of mud outdoors for Breezy to "muddy-
paw" into the house, making the kitchen floor gritty and
dulling her red-gold hair. Besides, I'd seen her hind foot
batting at her side too many times in the last few days
to doubt that fleas had moved in—in regimental numbers.

"Sorry, old girl."

Breezy had looked at me out of the corners of her eyes
as if she knew what was coming and was casting a solid
vote against it. Suspiciously, she trailed me to the base-
ment, her nails clicking on the linoleum floor behind me,
and watched disapprovingly while I carried the stack of
old towels upstairs to the bathroom and got out some scis-
sors for cutting away the knotted tangles of hair.

There was the usual tumult and struggle as I ran Breezy
down, coaxed her into the bathroom, then lifted and shoved
her over the edge of the tub. (It was remarkable how her
knees always locked in that no-bend position!) I'd lathered
her with the awful-smelling, flea-killing soap from the tops
of her floppy ears to the tip of her immobile tail. In the
course of Breezy's ordeal—to which she finally submitted—I got thoroughly sudsed myself.

After I'd lathered and lathered, rinsed and rinsed, then
toweled her dry and patted the tip of her nose with a
"There now, that wasn't so bad, was it?" she still glared
at me. The moment the door was open, she bounded out
like a schoolboy released from class at the ringing of the
three o'clock bell.

Breezy was gorgeous again, her long red hair shining,
her former flea population as drowned as Pharaoh's army
in the Red Sea. But the bathroom proclaimed that disaster
had struck. And I knew better than to venture a look in
the mirror at myself. I could feel a wet glop of suds strag-
gling my hair, dripping down my neck, and my jeans were

thoroughly soaked. Heaving a sigh of relief that at least it was over, I mopped the floor, the walls and me, thinking how like Breezy I'd been at times when the Lord dealt with me for my own good. Oh, how mightily I've resisted the work of the heavenly Vinedresser!

One of my commentaries told me I wasn't alone in resisting God. When I read, "All that is noble in us has been hammered into us by the hard things we would eliminate, against which we angrily protest," I knew it was true for me.

And yet afterward I've often been able to see the good, just as Breezy had hours later sidled up to me affectionately—after the loving care she didn't really want was over—full of forgiveness. She'd pressed her head into my hand as if to say, "I love you—and I know that awful bath was for my good. If you have to, give me another one when I need it again."

"Oh yes, Father," I prayed out loud. "I have resisted You—far worse than Breezy. But please keep working on me. Don't ever leave me to myself. I want to become all that You have planned for me."

A few days later, tucked inside a letter from a friend in California who knew about my new book project, was a simple poem she'd clipped from a magazine that summed it up so beautifully:

> Freshly grafted
> eager branch
> intently
> restlessly
> striving to
> bear fruit—
> how bitterly
> I felt
> the pruning shears
> and longed
> to break free
> to bloom

on my own.
Yet wisely,
graciously, Lord,
You denied me
the freedom
to become
a tumbleweed
or
piece of kindling.*

* "Recalcitrant Branch" by Barbara Penwarden, from DECISION, © 1976
by The Billy Graham Evangelistic Association.

Every branch of Mine that bears no fruit, He [the Vinedresser] takes away . . .

Withered Branches

Lord, those are hard words about taking away branches which bear no fruit. Instead of discovering what they mean I'd like to ignore this part of the Vine teaching and go on to the warm promises that follow. Yet I can't ignore words that sting, like them or not. You love me too much to let me get away with picking and choosing what I want to believe.

In the world of nature, there is probably no plant with so many weak and worthless branches as the vine. Since these lifeless branches are not fulfilling their purpose of fruit-bearing, they need to be taken away because they are a burden to the vine and to its sibling branches. They milk potent nutrients and give back nothing. They may overshade the rest of the plant and even provide a point of entrance for disease that can invade the whole structure. An unproductive branch is such a liability and risk that the vinedresser has no choice in the matter—it has to go, for the good of all.

30

Threatening as the words were, I needed to know what Jesus was talking about here. My prayer for insight into these verses led me to William Barclay's commentary. He explained that when Jesus was talking about the fruitless branches, He was referring to three kinds of people: those who refuse to listen to Jesus at all; those who listen to Him and render lip service only; and those who accept Him and then abandon Him.

I thought first of someone I had known—a woman who was a very talented business administrator with a large corporation. Shirley's salary was high, and she traveled with a crowd that was impressed with money, power and position. Then, as she told it, someone framed her, and she lost her job. For her, it was a mighty tumble, an earth-shaking disaster.

We had lunch together a couple of times and talked about God—the difference between His values and the values of our society today, the way He can salvage any life and use any situation when the life and situation are put into His hands. At first Shirley seemed interested, but every time we met, the bitterness she held in her heart against the people who had wronged her would erupt in some way. Finally I erupted and said, "Shirley, there's no way God can bless your life the way He wants to until you are willing to give up your bitterness and forgive the people you feel hurt you."

She blinked, a bit stunned, and protested, "I have every right to be bitter! What they did was wrong!"

My heart sank. By one set of standards, she was right. But according to God's standards there is only one way we can know His forgiveness, His healing, His new and abundant life. We are called to forgive others and to turn away from bitterness. Shirley was not willing to do that. I can still see her sitting there, smartly dressed, her silver-frosted hair elaborately coiffed, hanging onto her rights with all her might as her chin trembled and her eyes brimmed with tears.

I wish I could report a happy ending to this story, but I can't. Shirley didn't call me much after that. Instead she went from group to group, church to church, always trying to find someone who could promise her all she wanted from God and at the same time join with her in justifying her bitterness.

She made an occupation out of nursing her grudge, hugging her hurt. It became her life, and today she is a sad, pathetic person—in and out of mental hospitals, going from doctor to doctor. Sometimes at night I wake and see her face. I ache for her and I pray. In refusing to go God's way of forgiveness she is letting her life wither away like a branch that has refused to bear fruit.

What I hope is that one day—before the "gathering" of the branches—Shirley will let go of the bitterness and let God heal her. For no matter how dry and brittle the branch, I believe in the possibility of its being restored. It takes a miracle, but God is altogether able—and eager— to do just that. He'll perform the miracle of restoration for any who submit again to the Vine.

As I recalled Barclay's explanation of that troublesome verse on fruitless branches, it seemed to me that my friend was one of those who refused to listen to Jesus. Yet the second category of people—those who do listen but render lip service only—brings the truth of this text uncomfortably close to home.

There have been times in my life when I have clearly discerned His way in a given situation—no fuzzy grayness but a direct "Thus saith the Lord"—and yet I have been sorely tempted to give lip service only and take the easy way out by refusing to get involved.

Some years ago there was a struggle going on in our community over the issue of open housing. Minorities would come to town to teach at a nearby university and they would find it difficult to find suitable housing. Houses were available—but not to them. Day after day I read about it in the newspaper, heard people discuss it on the street and shared the personal pain of those who were among the victimized. Agonizing with them, I prayed, "God, *do* something!"

One Sunday morning I prayed longer and harder than usual, imploring God to intervene in the situation. Looking back, I wonder how I expected Him to work: Did I envision a white-robed celestial messenger delivering a heavenly decree to those in power?

God did take action all right, but not like that. As I walked toward church from the parking lot that day, a woman known locally as a strong activist stopped me and asked if I would be part of a women's committee to work on the problem. The committee would be interfaith and interracial, she assured me. What she didn't say—but what we both knew—was that it would also be highly controversial. Emotions in town were running high—people were trying to protect their vested interests and the situation was getting volatile.

As I stood on the threshold of the church, the scriptures and the Spirit of our Lord's life made it unmistakably clear to me: we are not to stand on the sidelines and let someone else take all the risks. I sensed God was requiring me to do something practical about my concerns. Nevertheless, I resisted His call with both feet firmly planted.

"Yes, Lord, I know I asked You to do something. I asked You fervently this very morning, but oh, Lord, I didn't mean for You to do it *this* way. Not through me, Lord."

My heart pounded as a dozen "legitimate" excuses raced through my mind: *I'm too busy—I might have to be out of town. As the wife of a minister I shouldn't get involved in something so controversial.*

But I couldn't persuade myself that any of my excuses held water.

Then a further out occurred to me. Maybe I could avoid open involvement by telling the woman I could not serve on the committee but that I would pray. Yet, before I could make the suggestion, I saw clearly that I was looking

for a way to ease out of an assignment God had for me.
In Barclay's words, I was "listening to Jesus and rendering
Him a lip service unsupported by deeds."

The seconds seemed forever as the woman waited pa-
tiently for my answer. Involvement could be dangerous,
I knew. But finally I said yes.

I *did* get involved. It *was* controversial. All of us on
the committee found ourselves at odds with certain members of the community. Some of my friends were outraged
when it became known that I was part of "the opposition."

Always, Louie had taught that a vital, personal faith
in Christ and an emphasis on social justice were two beats
of one heart. So during the time of this community crisis,
he preached on Colossians 3:11 and reminded us that there
is no more Jew nor Greek, slave nor free but that we
are one in Christ. Thus Christians could not be part of
excluding people from church or community on the basis
of race.

Even though most of our congregation endorsed this
concept of being involved in a whole gospel, there were
those who didn't.

After that sermon, we started getting hate mail. There
were obscene phone calls, and a few very vocal people
stormed at us to "get out and go to Harlem where you
belong." The thing that pained us most was a telegram
we received one day from 10 valued Christian friends. It
said in essence, "We love you, we want to remain your
friends, but please stick to the gospel and don't get involved
in these side issues."

But for us it was not a "side issue." Doing something
about our faith in this way was a vital part of living the
gospel. If we weren't willing to act on our convictions
we'd be guilty of being hearers of the Word and not doers,
and thus we would be deceiving ourselves as the Book
of James points out (James 1:22).

It was a painful period for our family—a time of being
stretched. We made mistakes, we hurt, we grew. But the

experience left us with an overall sense of peace in the eye of the storm. After the initial struggle, it also resulted in the congregation going on to become deeply involved in ministering to the needs of the whole person. We were learning to "walk the walk" as well as "talk the talk." Soon a widespread ministry of social justice involving 33 other churches was born—but not without considerable turmoil.

I share this experience only to show how perilously close I came to being a fruitless branch, a Christian whose Christianity consisted of profession without practice. It can happen so easily, so suddenly, as life confronts us with choices that test the practicality of our faith. For each of us the choices will be different, but when we sense God's direction and don't obey, we curtail fruitfulness. I read this week that when any living thing outgrows its useful function it is in danger of extinction. "The severest shock that any organism can sustain is a sense of uselessness," said Aldous Huxley.

Lord, I want to be useful. I want to bear fruit.

I remembered that Jesus made the same point in the parable of the fig tree in Luke 13. In effect He was saying, "These three years I have come seeking fruit, and I find none. You are overdue in terms of fruit-bearing."

Then God says to the Vinedresser, "No fruit? Cut it down! Why should it use up space on the ground?" But the Vinedresser pleads with Him, "Let me work with this plant one more year. Then if it does not bear fruit during the coming year, You can remove it from the vineyard."

The obvious message is that God will remove fruitless trees from the vineyard after a reasonable period of time. He will not continue to let them use up space or nourishment that could be utilized to bear fruit for Him. We are expected to bear fruit—or else! What a warning from the Lord!

How thankful I am that our Lord wants to work with us, on us, in us so that we can bear fruit. Admittedly,

the work can be painful to us—digging about the roots
of our life to make sure that we are firmly grounded in
Christ and not in any other person. But we can welcome—
or at least allow—His work in our lives when we know
it will enable us to fulfill our destiny of being fruit-bearers
for Him.

Scripture makes it clear to us that the primary cause
of fruitlessness in our lives is any conscious yielding to
sin. The late Dag Hammarskjöld spoke to this general principle in *Markings:* "You cannot play with falsehood without
forfeiting your right to the truth, play with cruelty without
losing your sensitivity of mind. He who wants to keep
his garden tidy, doesn't reserve a plot for weeds."

Years ago in another city I saw this principle at work
in Sally, a woman known for her loose relationships with
men. Although Sally was a churchgoer, she knew she was
not living in a way that honored God. There came a day
when she was sick of her life as it was, and she asked
me if I would pray with her. In the prayer, Sally made
her confession, asked for God's forgiveness and recommitted her life to Him.

There were no tears and little emotion. Sally was busi-
nesslike, but her prayer was not superficial. With a
determined manner, Sally thanked me and started toward
the door. "I have some work to do," she said.

"What do you mean?"

She smiled. "I'm starting a new life. The ties to the
old have to be cut. It means some telephone calls. Possibly
a few face-to-face confrontations."

There was a brief moment of hesitation. "Pray for me
that I'll be strong," she said softly.

Sally is a "do it now person" and knew she had to termi-
nate her wrong relationships quickly before she faltered.

A commitment to Christ means that everything that does
not honor God has to go to make room for the new life.
It is not that we will no longer sin but that we will no
longer consciously or intentionally yield to what we know

to be wrong. Nor, I remind myself, will we "chicken out" of responsibilities to which He has called us.

As dark—or disobedient—areas of our lives are taken away, there is more room for the inflowing of God's light, the presence of the love of Jesus, our Lord. Now that verse I had wanted to avoid was flooded with blessing in my understanding. I wanted it to apply to me. I wanted God to take away anything in my own life that did not honor Him. How good it was to know that our Vinedresser could be counted on to do that.

Several verses farther on Jesus seemed to underscore this point when He said, "If a man [person] does not abide in me, he is cast forth as a branch and withers; and the branches are gathered, thrown into the fire and burned" (John 15:6).

If the first verse was a threat to me, this one was even more so. Again I wanted to ignore it and go on to the "good parts" of the Scripture. But again the Lord had something to teach me here. Much as my mind wanted to reject its harshness, I somehow had to wrestle with the verse's plain speaking about what becomes of any of us who deliberately fail to continue to abide once we have been united to the Vine that is Christ.

That was Barclay's third category of fruitless branches— and I thought of Hugh and Helen, an attractive young Christian couple, richly endowed with talents and gifts from God. They had three delightful children and were active in various Christian groups within their community. Hugh was a successful businessman who also served the Lord through the distribution of inspirational pamphlets and tapes.

And then something happened. His zest for Christian work waned. To many he seemed to be just going through the motions. I later learned why. Hugh had become involved with an attractive, young widow. When confronted with this, he indignantly stated that he still loved his wife. But he also had a clear word from God, he said, that he

was to take care of this widow. To incredulous friends
and family he cited Old Testament passages where men
of God had more than one wife.

Then to their further consternation, he proceeded to
divide his time between two homes as though there was
nothing wrong with the arrangement. He even thought
his wife ought to be "unselfish" enough to accept the situation and be friendly to the other woman.

When the men in his fellowship group went to Hugh
and tried to reason with him, he wouldn't listen. He kept
insisting that he was solidly in the will of God.

Eventually Helen left Hugh, taking the children with
her. I don't know if there's been a divorce or not, for
Hugh has now cut himself off from all his Christian
friends. Deep down, he must be miserable; on the other
hand, it's hard to understand his trying to reconcile the
will of God with such behavior. A half-forgotten Bible
verse runs through my mind, reminding me that even the
very elect may be deceived (Matthew 24:24). Such things
can happen when branches fail to abide in the Vine. It
is only by God's grace we don't all get off the track—
perhaps not as blatantly as Hugh or as stubbornly as Shirley who refused to listen to God and let go of her bitterness.
But we are all vulnerable in some area of our lives.

I decided that John 15:6 still wasn't a happy verse, but
it was a very necessary one. It was the statement of an
inevitable truth: If we do not abide in the Vine Who gives
us life, we will be destroyed. And it is not His destruction
of us, it is our destruction of ourselves.

. . . and every branch that does bear fruit He prunes, that it may bear more fruit.

Pruning

Lord, what are You saying to me with the above verse? I can understand your pruning things out of my life that don't belong there. But do you mean I have to cut out some good things, too?

Was such a thing true of the natural grapevine? I wondered. Did vinedressers prune away "good" parts of the vine as well as "bad," unproductive parts?

Definitely yes. My research tells me that after the harvest, fruit-bearing branches are drastically cut back. And even before the harvest, some developing grape clusters are removed to ensure the highest quality of those that remain. The whole purpose of pruning is to enable the vines to grow the best possible grapes.

Suddenly I recalled a time when drastic pruning had taken place in my own life. It was needed for my very survival, though I certainly didn't realize it at the time and, like Breezy facing her bath, I fought it every step of the way.

39

It happened back in the late 1950s when Louie and I had been asked to start a new church in Bel Air, an area in the hills above Los Angeles. It was an exciting challenge—our first pastorate—and we both dived in full of enthusiasm. That the church had nowhere to meet except in the living room of our low, gray, California-style frame house on Roscomare Road didn't present any problems to me—at first. We kept 150 folding chairs in the garage for our weekly meetings and used the front bedroom for a church office. There was always plenty of excitement, the house being located at a too-sharp turn in the road. In one year 10 accidents happened in front of our house— some of them in the street, some in our front yard—when people didn't quite make the turn.

The backyard held its share of excitement too. It dropped off into Stone Canyon where the children joyously made forts and clubhouses. Lots of wildlife lived there too— rabbits, deer, coyotes and snakes. I remember well the day a coral king snake slithered through the open glass sliding doors into our living room and startled some parishioners sitting there.

After a while the growing congregation was able to rent the local elementary school auditorium for its Sunday morning worship service, but other meetings continued to be held in our home. It was almost a full-time job for me setting up chairs and taking down chairs, keeping the house straight for the meetings, baking cookies and making punch and coffee for refreshments. I had also agreed to be the Community Chest director for our area and accepted speaking invitations whenever possible. I was literally running from one "good" project to another.

Most demanding of my time and energy were our four babies, all under five years of age. I could never quite finish folding one load of clean diapers before it was time to begin another.

One night after all the church people had left, I dragged myself to our room and fell into bed utterly exhausted, thankful for a chance to rest. The rest was terribly short-lived, however. A stirring from the cradle put me on notice that our youngest was ready for his midnight feeding. As I picked him up, sat down in the gold brocade rocker and began to nurse him, I looked over at Louie sleeping soundly, looking *so* comfortable, and I felt a sudden flood of resentment. Why couldn't he be of more help to me! Well, of course I knew he couldn't nurse the baby, but I was bone tired, and I had to blame somebody for something. That attitude didn't honor God, but it was honest. Something needed pruning from my life, all right. The truth was hammered home when I went to see my doctor, who also was a close family friend, for a checkup a few days later.

"To be truthful, I'm really tired," I told him when he asked me how I'd been feeling.

"No wonder," he said, reading the lab report in front of him. "You're exceptionally anemic right now. I should put you in the hospital to see if we can build you up a little."

"But, Frosty!" I sputtered to our longtime friend. "Who would take care of the babies, the prayer breakfasts, the other meetings in our house, and the speaking engagements and the housecleaning and the Community Chest and. . ." I was about to run out of breath. "You just can't put me in the hospital!"

He sat there shaking his head. "Do you have any household help?" he asked when I had finished.

I had to laugh at his question. "Help? On a National Missions salary? There's no way."

"You're crazy, absolutely crazy," he muttered under his breath. "Another martyr mother who doesn't know how to take care of herself. Four babies, all that church work, and you still say yes to everybody who asks you to do anything. You'll be burned out before you're 40 if you keep that up."

That stern, no-nonsense lecture convinced me that if I

didn't make some immediate changes in my life, he'd be
forced to make them for me. In the meantime, though
he didn't put me in the hospital, he did schedule me for
twice-weekly visits to his office for shots of iron and vita-
min B-12. As I drove home through the heavy Los Angeles
traffic, I felt depressed. I thought Louie would be disappointed when I told him I couldn't keep on doing all the
things I had been doing to help in the ministry. Instead
he was wonderfully supportive. And I saw that he wasn't
the one who was pushing me to do so many things; they
were my own expectations for myself. What Louie really
wanted was for me to be the person God created me to
be—and to be able to enjoy him and the children.

I began praying that God would send help for all my
burdens. I asked Him to show me what I should do with
my schedule. As I prayed, I didn't say in so many words,
"Lord, what I really need is a maid, like many of my neigh-
bors have. Please send me one." But the thought was there,
churning inside me.

If He had sent a maid to help fold diapers and dust
furniture, I'd have continued in the disobedience of not
making Him the Lord of my daily routine. Instead, He
sent a shocking insight: my priorities were wrong. For
this season of my life, I was not meant to be out serving
every good cause but staying at home taking care of my
family, enjoying them and bearing fruit there. Instead of
a maid, judicious pruning was His answer to my prayer.
I wasn't supposed to try to please everyone. His was to
be the only opinion that mattered to me, and I was to
make Christ alone, and not other people, the Lord of my
life. That meant some changes.

As I embarked on the new life style, I began saying
no to a lot of good things. At the same time, I said yes
to some people who had been wanting to help me with
refreshments for meetings. And I said yes to a sweet-roll-
and-coffee prayer breakfast for the men instead of hurrying

to prepare bacon and eggs and toast for 20 people while
the baby was crying for attention.

It was the beginning of a real pruning of the old do-
it-myself syndrome that had been an element of unhealthy
pride in my life. And there was a lot more fruit-producing
fellowship to be gained when I asked others to help. I
even learned to stop inviting couples over for a supper I
had to cook—we made it potluck. That was the widening
of the door to let more people into my life.

In the months that followed, when someone asked me
to take on a responsibility I felt was not the Lord's plan
for me, I was free to say, "Thank you very much for thinking of me, but I just don't have the time right now. This
isn't the season yet for that kind of work in my life."

I didn't have to think I was Superwoman, and I didn't
have to feel guilty for turning people down. I was able
to stop condemning myself and chafing at the bit because
of the limitations of my strength and circumstances. In
fact, by cutting back, what I did brought greater joy and
was of more lasting value, both for me and for the other
people in my life. When we try to bear fruit in one season
that is meant for several seasons the fruit becomes bland,
even spoiled, lacking in richness and quality.

*Lord, why is it that many wives have such trouble yielding
to this kind of pruning, especially pastors' wives?* It seems we're
forever trying to live up to the unrealistic expectations
others have for us. Are they, perhaps, confusing us with
the One we serve? And do we allow—even encourage that?

At a luncheon one day I was seated next to the wife
of a man who had been a prominent minister in a large
city. He had built a huge congregation through his gifts
of teaching and preaching. But after many years, he had
left the pastorate for a church-related business which held
a new kind of challenge for him.

"How is it going?" I asked his wife. "How do you feel?
After all those years in the pastorate it must seem really

different for you two not to be serving a congregation."

"Oh, we miss the pastorate a lot," she said in an off-handed way, not caring who heard her. Then, after looking around to make sure people were no longer listening, she leaned close to my ear and whispered, "But there are compensations. For the first time in—I hate to say how many years—I don't feel guilty when we go out at night."

While she and her husband were serving a church, she went on to explain, no matter what they did in the evening, she was always aware of several other things they were supposed to be doing at the same time—attending this meeting or that one, visiting someone in the hospital, representing the church at some function, asking the invocation at a banquet.

Listening to her recital, I was newly aware that submitting to the Vinedresser's pruning is the only answer. People, being people, will always be encouraging us to bear more fruit than we're able to bring to maturity.

Yet, to be honest, we know it isn't only other people who push us into the barrenness of the too-busy life. We do it to ourselves—and sometimes at the expense of missing the full impact of some of life's most precious moments.

A few weeks before her recent wedding, our daughter, Andie, came to our room late one night and parked herself in "my chair." It was a welcome, quiet moment amid the flurry of dinners, parties, teas and showers. Ecstatic over marrying Craig, she was nevertheless weary and subdued—and very thoughtful.

"It's such a happy time, Mom," she said, "but please pray that I'll not be so busy I won't be aware of all the feelings and the depth of what is *really* happening."

Ah, yes, Andie. Wise girl that you are, you know that even happy, good things must sometimes be trimmed back in order that we may be—and may stay—aware of what is real. One of the benefits of careful pruning is that it gives us the time we need to love—and to be authentically aware.

In our limited way of looking at things, we might fail to see the necessity for pruning a particular branch, but God knows what's really needed there. An illness that slows us down, frustrated plans or a door slammed in our face—all these can be evidence of His love and care. His judgment can be trusted to make sure that the vineyard will fulfill its purpose of productivity. And what is our part in this? To submit—simply and profoundly—to His wisdom and love, offering ourselves to Him for whatever He wants to do.

Many times we will find ourselves submitting to the pruning away of some very good things to make way for the best, because if there is too much developing fruit, the branch will be weakened, and none of it will reach maturity. Furthermore, too much fruit can literally break a branch that is not strong enough to bear such a load, as I came near discovering.

My friend, Catherine Marshall LeSourd, is one of the most refreshingly honest persons I know. Though she sometimes makes me say "Ouch!" she is one of the friends to whom I go when I need a straight answer. She is equally honest with herself about her own schedule, knowing she has to "abide in her call." By its fruit of changed lives, writing is clearly her priority. Since she also has a major talent in speaking, Catherine is tempted to fragment the use of her time and energy with too many public appearances and social events.

But it is not only writers and leaders—the "busy people"—who have to wrestle with decisions between the good and the best in order to abide in their call. All of us—homemakers, people in business, labor, government, blue collar, white collar—we all need to see our priorities, our calls, and let God prune our lives by guiding our yeas and nays.

Nancy and Jim Johnson are good friends of ours from Fort Collins, Colorado, now living in Washington while Jim serves the fourth district of his state in the U.S. House of Representatives. Our two families moved to Washington at about the same time, and we met one Sunday after church. As we chatted we discovered that we had much in common—children of the same ages, two of them freshmen at the same college—and many similar interests and values. One of the most important bonds between us was a decision we shared to keep our basic commitments to our families.

Since the social life of Washington is a constant round of receptions and parties, many people get caught up in them to the point where their families become classic examples of neglect. It is a doubly hazardous track for a congressman and his wife who have not only extraordinary demands during the week but are pulled back to their districts on the weekends. During one of the times when our two families got together, I remember hearing Jim say, "There's just so much of a price I'll pay for this job, and being away from my family every weekend is not part of it."

Although Jim wouldn't phrase it this way, he was clearly declaring his intention to abide in his call as a father and a husband. Though it hasn't been easy, he has stuck to that decision for all the years they have lived in both Colorado and Washington. A heart-clutching postscript to this situation is something Nancy told me about recently as we shared a huge burrito (Mexican food is a mutual passion), during a visit together at our home.

It was an election year in 1978, and the Johnsons had to spend time campaigning. It meant that their youngest child, Drake, who was in school in Washington, had to spend more time than usual alone. As election day drew near, Jim had to be away from home for two weeks straight. Then, after the election, one of his colleagues, Congressman Leo Ryan, invited Jim to join him on a fact-finding tour of Jonestown in Guyana.

Jim's answer was an immediate, "No, I've been away long enough. I've got to get back to my boy."

Because of the horrible massacre that took place in Jonestown and the death of some of those on the fact-finding tour, Nancy is profoundly grateful for Jim's faithfulness to his priorities.

Catherine, Nancy and Jim—each in a unique way—have helped me to understand the importance of perceiving my own true calling in the Lord at a given time so I can cooperate with the Vinedresser's pruning process.

I also learned that some pruning of the grapevine is to allow buds to develop that were previously dormant because they had been dominated by the "tip bud." The application seems to be that when pruned of one prominent characteristic or activity we may be surprised to find other concealed talents and gifts coming to fruition.

I have seen that happen. We are snipped or pinched in one place—perhaps hurt by words or thoughtless deeds—and that has allowed our latent ability to forgive to come forward, also revealing in us a quality of tenderness. Or we are nipped by illness and thus have to draw on resources of patience and faith we never knew we had. Pruning sometimes lays bare our needs in such a way that we're able to allow others into our lives on a deeper, more honest level. I have seen doors of opportunity slam shut in more than one friend's face only to see them find their real calling, the one that would bear the most fruit, in some other vocation.

There have been times in my life when I realized that a particular pruning was a blessing, enabling me to bear more and better fruit. There have been other prunings in which I cannot yet see the good. But I know that whatever my feelings, I can trust God, our heavenly Vinedresser to prune me correctly when I am abiding in the Vine.

Jesus makes it clear, however, that it is the Father who does the pruning—not us. When we usurp His role and try to trim one another's lives we're asking for trouble. It can easily become manipulation, actually playing God in the life of another.

For example we are to discipline our children—but taking care that we don't crush their spirits (Ephesians 6:4). Yes, there is a time to admonish the unruly (1 Thessalonians 5:14)—but then Paul also tells us to encourage the fainthearted, help the weak and be patient with all. We'd best beware that in our zeal to help one another we don't neglect to accept, love and encourage one another to greater fruitfulness. If as children of the Vinedresser we take the sharp pruning shears in our own, eager hands, we may cut too much or cut in the wrong place. Our bumbling attempts may leave another's life shorn of essential vitality so that it would take years to return to peak fruitfulness. We can even render permanent damage.

We'd do better to make our views known to the Vinedresser in prayer and then let Him cut away what most needs to go.

Even with the most skillful pruning, bleeding or loss of sap still can occur in the grapevine. Some of this is necessary; it is the bleeding sap, the "tears" plugging over the pruned wood, which protects it from disease invaders while it is being healed.

Yes, Lord, I can see how in my own life You've allowed sorrow— even with tears—to accompany pruning, but it has always worked ultimately for my good.

Let me share with you a poem I've found meaningful, written by Allegra McBirney whose books and radio ministry have touched many for Christ.

Lord, I got this booklet, GUIDE TO PRUNING,
Supposedly to learn about my plants;
But it turns out that I have learned far more about
You as the Vine, me as a branch, the Father as the Gardener
Than I have learned about my garden's care!

I've seen that all these testings lately
And the tears that I've been through
Have really been the pruning knife and not the rod.

My GUIDE TO PRUNING says that "cutting back
Will head off growth in wrong directions."
Now I see that through these trials
You've done exactly that!
There were some wrong directions, weren't there, Lord?

It also says,
"Good pruning cuts the shoots that sap the strength."
And surely my distractions sapped me of the strength
And time—and love—that should have gone to You!
I needed Your professional attention!

You know, I used to think that all this "cutting back"
Was wrecking me
But now I see that it has "forced new growth!"
You knew it would!
Now make me bear much more—and sweeter—fruit . . .

I see at last Your purpose in my tears:
Your pruning was to bring my branch perfection,
Not destruction.

Your GUIDE TO PRUNING is Your Love . .

The cutting back was painful, and yet through it all
I felt Your closeness in a very special way;
And now I know the Gardener is never quite so near
The branch as when with His own hand
He's pruning it . . .*

---

* "Guide to Pruning" by Allegra McBirney from *Interest* magazine, June 1976.

*You are already made clean by the
word which I have spoken to you.*

Cleansed Branches

"Not me, Lord," I was tempted to say after reading
the above words. "I'm not that clean yet, and neither are
most of the other people I know. I guess You were talking
to Your disciples here, the ones who had walked with You
and lived intimately with You on this earth. You were
saying that Your teaching had made them clean. But to
be honest I still feel that I fall short."

The truth is that I don't know of anyone who has been
"made clean" totally. We are all in process at one point
or another.

I know a truly beautiful human being with enormous
gifts of personality. But like all of us she is flawed. There
is a volatile streak in her disposition that, as she has grown
older, has become more pronounced and energy-draining.
A lost date book or pair of glasses, or a red light at a
corner when she is in a hurry (which is almost always),
can set off a tirade. When we are together for any length

of time I get weary just witnessing the emotional outbursts. I can imagine how drained she must feel, being the site where the explosions take place.

Recently God has been speaking to her about all the lost energy that really belongs to Him, and she has decided she doesn't want to be this way for the rest of her days. In obedience to God, she is consciously and deliberately submitting this area of her life to Him for cleansing. When she feels an explosion brewing she prays and submits— again and again.

The habit is deep, and the cleansing must be deep as well. Yet the Vinedresser is loving and skilled, equipped in every way to deal with diseased branches. It may take a while, but I see and feel a difference in her already. She is a powerful personality with a driving desire to live her life fully for God. I think of her when I read, ". . . let us also lay aside every weight, and sin which clings so closely, and let us run with perseverance the race that is set before us" (Hebrews 12:1).

In submitting her irascible nature to God for cleansing and healing, my friend is laying aside a weight that has slowed her pace. I'm sure we all have some laying aside to do. Some of us need to be cleansed of painful memories and emotional scars. These can drain us even more than physical demands. When we are carrying internal burdens we wake in the morning and feel weary before our day has even begun. Unforgiveness of those who have hurt us can eat away our energy as we sleep. Cleansing and healing are needed here too. How does it come? It may be through a Scripture passage suddenly brought to life for us by the Spirit. We may sense His inner voice speaking to our hearts. It often comes through the love and insight of family or friends. Yet, as Jesus has made clear, regardless of how we are made clean, it will be consistent with His Word to us in Scripture.

In my own life, there was a painful situation which could have put a heavy emotional burden on me if God my Vinedresser had not cleansed me of it in a beautiful way.

My parents were divorced when I was about two years old. Because my mother and I had gone to live with her father, I had hardly been aware of missing a father because both of these primary people in my life were so loving and committed to me. But if I hadn't felt somehow deprived, why did my memory still hold a picture of me as a little girl sidling up to a strange man at a picnic, hoping the other children would think he was my daddy?

I saw my natural father very rarely—once when I was 12 years old, another time when I was 19. Both encounters were so brief that, had it not been for a few yellowed photographs, I doubt I would have remembered what my father looked like. Later there were a few other contacts, but again they were always brief and separated by many years. These had not been traumatic experiences for me and I was not aware of any underlying emotional current that needed to be steadied.

But when I was 38 years old and we were living in La Jolla, the phone rang one night and a barely familiar voice said, "Hello, Honey. This is your daddy."

The call caught me off guard. My father had remarried, and he and his wife were coming to San Diego where he was going to be speaking at a convention. He wanted Louie and me to have dinner with them.

My reaction surprised me. Instead of being overjoyed to hear from him, there was a reservoir of hurt and indignation in me. If I had expressed it in words, it might have sounded something like, "Why now? After all these years, why are you now choosing to notice that I exist?"

I wanted to shove the unwelcome feelings back down where they came from, to refuse to face my father and risk a further stirring up of the deep hurt of which I had been almost totally unaware. But Louie insisted that we accept the invitation. And I knew he was right. In no way could I feel that God would encourage me to hide from facing a painful situation head on. The implications from Scripture were clear to me—not just one verse, but throughout—that with God's help I was to face life and all its challenges honestly and squarely.

Not only did Louie and I pray about the situation, but a group from our church gathered around me and offered prayers for my strengthening. That my tears flowed for a long time showed me there was a lot of emotional buildup of which I had been unaware.

As Louie and I drove to San Diego's Town and Country Inn to meet my father and his wife, my mind reviewed a host of questions I felt entitled to ask—unpleasant, challenging, guilt-triggering questions like, "Where were you all those years when I really needed you?"

But when we were actually together, seated at the table, a strange thing happened. All my questions were forgotten, and my desire to let him know how he had hurt me simply disappeared. Mostly, I just stared at him in wonder, drinking in what he looked like. His eyes were a remarkable blue, and when he turned his head toward Louie, giving me a full profile to study, I found myself thinking: *Ah-ha, so that's where my nose came from!*

I absorbed every feature, commenting inwardly with, strangely, a warm kind of thanksgiving while Louie and my father talked enthusiastically about many things. During a lull in my conversation with his gentle, lovely wife Lucille, I heard Louie ask my father how he happened to get started in the field of engineering. Why, I'd forgotten that he was an engineer—if I'd ever known.

Louie's questions were genuine, friendly questions. And in my father's responses, I learned that he had gone back to college after the divorce and that instead of being a drifter as I'd always supposed, he'd worked for the same company for more than 35 years. In his work, he'd been required to live all over the world. A real adventurer, I decided, and I found myself respecting—and liking—this person who was definitely a part of me.

He was a man who'd had deep needs in his own life, and suddenly I knew I didn't have to have answers to all my questions. I could forgive—and forget—the hurts that had been buried so long, and now I could enter into a new, enjoyable relationship with him and his wife. I could accept him right where he was that day, with no unforgiven memories to mar our friendship. What a much-needed cleansing that was!

We didn't see one another a lot after that, but we stayed in touch. My father's wife and I became friends: she was a person I found easy to love. We communicated at Christmas and other holidays; we telephoned them when we were in their part of the state, and they phoned when they came into our area. We made a point of seeing one another when the opportunity presented itself. Genuinely warm feelings developed between us.

About two years after that first dinner together, I received an urgent phone call from Lucille.

"Colleen, your father's terribly ill. Can you come?"

This time there was no hesitation. "Of course I can come. I *want* to come." Louie and I spent some hours with him in the hospital. Then there was a second visit. A very short time later another call came, this time to notify us that he had died.

How thankful I was that God had allowed this unhealthy shadow in my life to be revealed to me while there was still time for a healing reconciliation. Part of me could have been buried alive in a broken relationship. I was glad not to have that burden to carry.

Often we are not in touch with our real feelings about things. We bury them until painful circumstances expose the nerves. But when we become aware of the sensitive areas that need cleansing and healing, God our Vinedresser is always ready to help us.

For the natural vine, cleansing is not a once-and-forever thing that happens at a particular stage in the life of the vine. It's an ongoing process, a constant battle, and the vinedresser must always be on the alert to protect the vines and their branches from disease, insect pests and parasites. There are foes from without which blatantly devour the fruit or leaf or roots, and there are foes within which insidiously interrupt the chemical balances. The plant has some defense mechanisms of its own but the vinedresser has to take appropriate action against predators.

Some insects are camouflaged and hard to see; some parasites are so small they are virtually invisible and are not detected until after they have caused major injury to the plant.

What parallels are there to the life of the Christian? I wondered. Do we have similar problems? And if so, how can we combat them?

Parasites, sap-suckers—oh, yes! We all encounter those pests, the two-legged variety, who drain time and energy by selfish demands for attention and help while refusing to take responsibility for their own lives or to take any steps to be healed of the causes of their ills.

More virulent are those parasites who want to dominate people under the guise of religion. They infiltrate Christian groups and distort Scripture, using certain passages to attack other groups or persons. Some of these insects are easy to spot. Not so with others. At first they may seem harmless, even gifted and inspired by God. Yet, as their sphere of leadership grows—especially if there is no larger body to which they are accountable—they can subtly get off the track and use their position to mislead and exercise the kind of power over others that properly belongs only to God.

The Bible is full of warnings about leaders who would try to take the place God has reserved for Himself alone. Had the members of the Jonestown cult followed Scripture instead of their sick and misguided leader, the tragedy of more than 900 deaths in Guyana—most of them suicides or forced suicides—would never have occurred.

The front-page news stories about Jonestown reminded me how the Word cleanses us and keeps us from excesses that do not honor God—even though they may spring from good motivations. However, we should not sit in judgment on the people of the Jonestown community, for in their tragedy we can see that there is a fine line between reality and unreality, wholeness and sickness, truth and falsehood.

My probing of the 15th chapter of John was giving me a new vision of God's call on my life. He wanted me to have His Word so embedded in me, and my obedience to it so firmly established, that I would be a cleansed branch, freed from the grip of any blight or parasite that could impede my growth.

I'm not there yet, Lord—but yes, that's what I want, too!

Abiding

When Jesus says, "Abide in Me, and I in you," He invites us to share life with Him on the deepest level.

Lord, deepen my understanding of this gracious invitation. I have a feeling there is a powerful implication here for my life.

My dictionary tells me that the word "abide" means to "remain with, to reside with, to await, to endure, to stand fast, to go on being, to be submitted, to continue without change." As I slip the dictionary back into its niche in the book shelf, our son, Jamie, passes by and contributes, "Mom, to me, abiding in Jesus means to hang in there with Him. Even when it's tough and discouraging, we don't give up."

I like that.

From a more theological perspective, Thomas Merton says, "Abiding is a consciousness of our union with God, of our complete dependence on Him, for all our vital acts in the spiritual life, and of His constant, loving presence in the depths of our souls . . ."

What a difference between an "out-there-somewhere God" and One who abides within, offering me a personal, intimate relationship with Him.

I see the difference—but I don't always live the difference in my everyday life.

For instance, I often "fritter and fret" abiding right out the window. I'm an expert at frittering (as in "frittering my time away"), and fretting (as in "fretting over little things"). Too often I spend time and energy fretting over all I have to do, making lists and feeling exhausted simply anticipating what is to come. At other times I simply put it all before the Lord, praying that He will engineer events, make the crooked places straight and give me the energy and help I need one day at a time. It's amazing when I let my schedule abide in Him how much easier everything becomes. When I cease fretting today about tomorrow, today is wonderfully taken care of.

How many hours of sleep we miss because we become anxious and fretful over the little things—and sometimes the not-so-little things. But it comforts me to remember that Paul confessed to "many a sleepless night." He knew real fear and depression, but he didn't justify them or stew in them. He continued to pray to be delivered and shared with us his answer: "Don't worry over anything whatever; tell God every detail of your needs in earnest and thankful prayer, and the peace of God, which transcends human understanding, will keep constant guard over your hearts and minds as they rest in Christ Jesus" (Philippians 4:6–7, PHILLIPS).

So my real question is, how can I abide by resting my heart and mind in Christ Jesus more consistently?

And what about other abiders, Lord? How do they do it? How do they keep on abiding and being obedient in the midst of the frustrations of the day? Would their methods work for me?

I thought of the conversation I'd had with Jamie just a few days ago when I had come downstairs before he left for the day. I'd found him at the family-room table with his Bible open and his notes ringed around his cereal bowl.

"Jamie, I really respect that in you," I'd said, nodding toward the array before him. "You're more disciplined than any of the rest of us."

"Sure, Mom," he'd said, "because I have to be. I'm still new at all this. I can't abide during the day unless I get in gear to start with."

I was impressed that his attitude was not—as mine might have been—a judgmental, "Yeah, and that's what everyone else in this house should be doing too." He simply had a practical awareness that he was doing what he needed to do to stay close, connected and abiding.

I knew that some abiders seasoned by time and habit have learned to pray as they work and go from place to place. (My husband goes through his prayer list as he does his exercises to start the day; he also has short, set-apart times in the afternoon and evening.) But it's a problem to find that oasis in the midst of a fully scheduled life.

And then suddenly I was remembering a day when our children were little. The house was full of noisy, happy confusion, and bedlam threatened to take over. Louie's mother, Marie Evans, was visiting us at the time. She is such a Godly woman, serene in any storm. I asked her, "Mother, when life is this busy and chaotic, how do you find time to pray?"

She was able to reply immediately without having to think about it, because the answer was *real* in her life. "You watch for the first quiet opportunity, Coke," she said. "You may not be able to set a time, but you can be on the watch for it, and recognize it when it comes along. For me, it used to be in the morning, when Daddy had left for the church and the older children had headed for school. As soon as I got the baby down for a nap, I'd take time to be with the Lord."

Even today, when Mother Evans is with me the instinct is there. When things slow down for a minute—people leave, and the phone isn't ringing—I'll see her stop work to listen and pray.

"Shh," she'll say. "Just listen to this quiet house." And the next words that come from her mouth are always, "Cokey, let's pray."

Mother Evans had to learn this secret of abiding—and put it into practice every day—she told me, because her life was one that was almost frantic with activity. In the midst of it, she had to seize every opportunity to pray, and she did, without ever thinking she had to go away to some outside retreat to do it.

Somewhere I'd read about a tiny woman who lived back in the 1700s in a house jammed with children. She must have been something like Mother Evans. Since there was no way she could leave the children to go away from the house for a quiet time (and yet she knew she had to have her times with the Lord or forfeit something special in their relationship), she made her own very private prayer closet in the midst of bedlam by pulling several layers of her voluminous skirts up over her head. The children learned to respect that as a sign they weren't to interrupt her unnecessarily; they knew she was spending time with her God. It made a difference in her life—and in the lives of her children. How wonderful! Too bad we don't have that many layers of petticoats in the twentieth century.

And then I remembered Brother Lawrence. Surely he hadn't needed petticoats. His name is almost synonymous with his intriguing work *The Practice of the Presence of God.* A Frenchman of lowly birth, Brother Lawrence was converted to God at the age of 18 when he looked upon "a dry and leafless tree standing gaunt against the snow." It stirred deep thoughts within him of the change the coming spring would bring. From that moment on he grew strong in the love and favor of God, endeavoring constantly, as he put it, "to walk in His presence." For the rest of the 80 years of his life, Brother Lawrence served his fellow Carmelite monks as a cook in Paris where he died in 1691.

First applying himself to prayer, Brother Lawrence would go to the kitchen to begin his duties at the appointed time (*just like me, Lord*), praying, "O my God, since Thou art with me, and I must now, in obedience to Thy commands, apply my mind to these outward things, I beseech Thee to grant me the grace to continue in Thy presence; and to this end do Thou prosper me with Thy assistance . . ."

Right there I saw something I'd never seen before in Brother Lawrence's account. He hadn't "practiced the presence" on his own, he'd prayed and asked God for "grace to continue," invoking *His* assistance. So that's how he did it. By God's enabling. What a revelation!

But would that prayer work for me, too? Would such a prayer enable me to stay in God's presence in the midst of "frittering and fretting" and everyday frustrations?

I knew from his later testimony that Brother Lawrence's prayer was answered for him above all he could ask or think. Again, I read the much loved words aloud: "The time of business does not with me differ from the time of prayer."

Could that be true for me? I read on. "And in the noise and clatter of my kitchen, while several persons are at the same time calling for different things, I possess God in as great tranquillity as if I were upon my knees at the blessed sacrament."

How remarkable. Brother Lawrence could abide in the Lord's presence in his kitchen at the same time several people were calling for his services. Did these interruptions frustrate him? Obviously not. His job in the kitchen was to serve others. It was the Lord's presence amidst obvious confusion that gave him such spectacular grace.

Lord, I pray that You will grant me, too, the grace to continue to abide in You without interruption in my kitchen, and as I deal with the inevitable frustrations of daily life.

If abiding makes the difference in common frustrations, how much more we feel the impact of abiding when life's major events—both glad and sad—come crashing in upon us. For some reason, this morning my mind embarked on a nostalgic journey as I pondered, one by one, the life passages I have gone through since starting this book. Again and again I have taken pen in hand to begin to write—only to lay it down as my life was engulfed in a passage that consumed me totally. First, my mother's unexpected death, where I experienced a depth of loss and mourning unlike any I've known to this time. But life continues, and within six months, not only I but the whole family was caught up in the joy of our daughter's engagement and marriage to a man we all loved. Another passage. Next, as though in answer to his longing to "be with Stella," my stepfather fell gravely ill and died just a year after my mother's sudden passing.

Then, more recently, there was a warning to Louie about his too-pressured life. We both so believe in the abiding principle that a year ahead in our date books we schedule times for rest and relaxation, times to get away from what someone has called "the tyranny of the urgent." These are also occasions for self-examination to see if we are in God's rhythm of abiding.

Yet again and again the days marked, "time away for quiet and rest," get replaced by events that seem more important to us at the time. Our zeal to be about the Lord's business, however, is no excuse, if in the process we are becoming unhealthy branches.

Fatigue started to build up in Louie during the Lenten season. He asked for a week of post-Easter study-rest leave which the church gladly granted. By then it was too late. When we arrived at the mountain cabin we had rented, my husband was really ill. His tired, run-down body had yielded to acute infectious hepatitis.

The doctor ordered Louie to take six weeks away from work for a complete rest. If it couldn't be done at home, he threatened to put him in the hospital. It was a painful lesson. When we failed to exercise wisdom about our life style, God had intervened. So after only two days at the cabin, we returned home for an enforced season of quiet

But how much we learned about abiding in those six weeks. In His sovereignty and love, God "made us lie down," and by the third week of rest, we were luxuriating "in His green pasture." We had time to worship Him, time for each other, time for others and time to immerse ourselves in study and contemplation of the Word.

Frank Laubach, who brought literacy to millions, once said, "My job here . . . is to live wrapped in God." I know now what he means, for through the pain and joy of these experiences, I have felt an abiding presence so real, so powerful, that I have felt literally "wrapped in God."

As I thought more about His powerful presence in times of need, a whole new aspect of this abiding relationship began to unfold.

Where is His presence? I asked myself, knowing the answer. It's never "out there somewhere." It's an "in-us" presence. Jesus is within us. We are the temples where His Holy Spirit dwells.

I'd known these things intellectually, but in these quiet weeks the words were filled with new significance. Jesus' words, "Abide in Me, and I in you," were not talking about two different things. Both phrases were talking about the same thing! We can't abide in Him unless He is already abiding in us! It is only the life of the Vine *in* the branch that makes the branch able to do anything— even to abide.

I realized I had been consciously or unconsciously striving to abide. How futile! My thoughts had been on abiding as a work we have to do, instead of on the living Christ in whom we were to be kept abiding. Abiding should contain no strain or effort; it is rest from effort. The natural branch certainly need not strain to remain a part of the vine; it simply is. All it need do is *stay* connected.

Put another way, it is not our faithfulness to discipline our lives that will enable us to live in Christ; but it is His faithfulness that makes us want to spend the time with Him. Therefore I don't have to struggle and strain to learn how to abide; I just have to rely utterly on Him.

The psalmist tells us how God provides not only sleep but provides for our needs even as we sleep. (See Psalm 127 in the Amplified Bible.) Brother Lawrence, writing to this same point, says, "The barque of the soul [or the vessel or boat that is the soul] goeth forward even in sleep." In other words, we can abide even as we rest at night.

As the branch abides in the vine, so does the Vine abide in His Father. ". . . I do nothing on my own authority but speak thus as the Father taught me." And further, "I speak of what I have seen with My Father, and you do what you have heard from your father" (John 8:28,38).

Jesus did what He saw His Father do. Jesus said what He heard His Father say. Abiding perfectly, He willed only the will of His Father. How true it was when He said, "I come to do Thy will, O God." And when I am truly abiding in Him, keeping in constant touch, practicing His presence, obeying His commands—by His grace I can say it, too!

When we abide in Him, we are promised many benefits: answered prayer, God's love, fruits, joy, friendship with God, the gift of the Comforter, the ability to witness. When I abide, the promises are fulfilled. But when I don't keep my part of the bargain—which is simply to trust God ultimately in the abiding process and to obey Him—the love and joy in my life begin to fade, and I begin to grumble. "All right, Lord, where are all those good things You promised?" My accusing tones make it sound as if the failure is in Him and not in me.

Then I'm brought up short to realize all over again that the promises are contingent promises. There are conditions attached: *If* you abide in Me—trusting Me to enable you; *if* you keep My commands—again, trusting Me to keep you faithful.

At that point, I look to see where I have gone wrong. My problem is often one of spiritual laziness, as I simply fall away from doing those things that keep me abiding in Christ. When I am not looking to God's strength to do a work in me, I let the demands of life usurp the time I've set aside for keeping my communion with the Lord up to date.

Jesus was always on call for real needs, but He also made sure that He had time with His Father. If we don't do this, too—if we let meaningless intrusions steal away the time meant for God—we won't know the power of abiding.

How easy it is to let the little demands of the world come in and nip away at our day, gobbling up any chance we might have for drawing close to Him and strengthening our abiding. Some of these little foxes can look very noble like responding to a call to serve, to be active, to be a helper—all good in themselves. Yet if we let them consume and control our time, we can shut out the Lord, not listening to Him, because we're so busy taking care of everyone else. And in the process, we become withered branches.

And so I am freshly and powerfully reminded that abiding has to come first in my life. As I abide, I will have so much more of value to share with the people I am to serve. Abiding is worth whatever it costs me in time. And as I abide in Him, I am becoming the person He intends me to be.

I am the Vine, you are the branches.
He who abides in Me and I in him,
he it is that bears much fruit, for
apart from Me you can do nothing.

Harvest

That it is God Himself who enables us to abide in Jesus so inspires me that it seems almost a letdown to be told that I am a branch which is to bear fruit. Yet I know I cannot neglect the harvest of the branches.

From my botanical notes I have learned that the sturdy trunk—the main, permanent woody part of the vine above the ground—is firmly established by a vigorous underground root system. In addition to lifting the branches to light and air, the trunk of the vine brings up water and minerals in its sap to the food-producing leaves and then distributes that food to all parts of the plant. Without the work of the vine there could be no branches, no leaves, no flowers, no fruit.

In the same way we, the branches, are lifeless without Jesus our Vine. As branches we have an indispensable role to fulfill—bearing fruit. Just as the natural vine cannot produce fruit except through the branches connected to it, so Christ's fruit is borne through you and me.

The amazing thought here is that while I know I'm dependent upon God my Creator, there is a real sense in which He needs me, too. What a remarkable and beautiful risk Jesus took in choosing to depend on us, His disciples, to be His fruit-bearers in the world.

Brimming up in me is a desire to fit perfectly into Jesus' plan for me as a branch and to bear the fruit for which He has designed me. And yet I know that eagerness to bear fruit won't produce fruit. Abiding will. "Without Me, you can do nothing," Jesus has told us. How plain it was that He had to always come first, and then the fruit would be inevitable.

Another fact about the vine is that without the life sap coursing through it, no branch can bear anything. *Is there a life-giving sap that flows through me, Lord, when I'm in an abiding relationship with You?*

In my study of Andrew Murray's *Abide in Christ* I discovered what I had suspected. The life sap for the Christian— the means by which Christ indwells the believer, providing all he needs for fruit production, is the Holy Spirit, the divine Enabler.

Right then I took a brief study course on the Holy Spirit to get Him out of the fuzzy, theological-jargon-land of my thinking and bring into focus His role in my life as a branch united to Jesus the Vine. We see Him all through the scriptures, beginning with the first chapter of Genesis where the Spirit moved on the face of the waters, all the way through the last chapter of Revelation where the Spirit and the Bride (Christ's true Church), say, "Come." Jesus told His disciples that it was better for Him to leave them and go to the Father so that He could send His Holy Spirit to be with all believers everywhere at all times (John 14:16).

There is a significance to the location of John 15. It

comes right after Christ's teaching on the Holy Spirit (in John 14), as the means by which God makes His abode in us, and then is followed by His teaching on the Holy Spirit as the One who *does* so many things in our lives (John 16).

It is the Holy Spirit inside us who makes us aware of our sin and need for Christ. Whether our being drawn to God is swift or slow is not the important point. That we do finally respond to this loving persistence of the Spirit, however, is crucial. Then His work can continue in our lives as children of God as He equips us with His gifts for ministering the grace of God to others—for bearing fruit.

The Holy Spirit is the means by which God abides in us and the means by which we abide in Him. The Holy Spirit is the life sap through which Jesus the Vine and we as branches grow into one and are held in union. The Holy Spirit is the living connection.

Having been reminded in a new way of who He is and what He does, I do not want to be guilty of neglecting the Person of the Holy Spirit. As a result, I have seen Him with fresh eyes at work in the lives of people who bear the fruit of the Spirit.

Several years ago Mother Teresa of Calcutta, India, was introduced to an overflow congregation at Washington's National Presbyterian Church which included people from every part of Christendom. It was the first time this saintly Roman Catholic had ever spoken in a Protestant church.

A tiny Albanian woman of God, dressed in a simple unbleached muslin habit with bands of faded blue on the edges, Mother Teresa stood simply at the front of the sanctuary and spoke briefly of the work of the Sisters of Charity among the poorest of the poor who are dying each day in the slums of Calcutta. It was in the name of these same people that she would accept the Nobel Prize for Peace in 1979.

We were all melted down by the love that shone from the depths of her eyes and spread over her care-lined, yet joyful face. I was not the only one in the congregation with tears as I listened to her softly spoken words about how blessed it is to live in poverty and to share the suffering of God's children. And I'll never forget the perfect way she summed it up, putting to shame forever all "good works" that don't originate in the heart of God: "It is not that you serve the rich or the poor. It is the love you put into the doing."

A part of the daily prayer of Mother Teresa and her co-workers goes like this: "Make us worthy, Lord, to serve our fellow men throughout the world who live and die in poverty and hunger. Give them through our hands their daily bread, and by our understanding give peace and joy."

Why did they pray to be "worthy" to serve the poorest of the poor? I wondered about this at first but not for long. In serving these unfortunates, the Sisters of Charity felt they were literally serving their Lord, the King of Kings. For according to His own words, "As you did it unto the least of these My brethren, you did it to Me," they *were serving Him*. No wonder Mother Teresa kept saying, "I see Jesus in the face of the poorest of the poor." No wonder they prayed to be worthy of this. And because she and the Sisters of Charity served with such tenderness and love, with every fruit of the Spirit being manifested in their ministrations, the "poorest of the poor" must see Jesus in their faces too!

After Mother Teresa had left the church and we were back in our home, Louie turned to me, his hands held out in an imploring gesture and said, "What are we going to do? I mean, what can we do with our lives that will answer this challenge?"

I had the same sense of inadequacy, but at the same time I felt gratitude that there are such laid-down lives, such unlimited poured-out love, such conscious, transparent dependence on the Vine for every act of mercy. And such union with Him!

Mother Teresa's visit made us newly aware that in our own community there were also hungry people, lonely people, needy people. We could not all go to India to feed and care for the starving millions, but we could do more than we were doing to give food and a cup of water in Jesus' name to the hungry in our own city; and to give time and money to the groups who are fighting injustice and meeting the physical needs of mankind.

One of the groups we became involved with was the ministry led by John Staggers who is associated with Fellowship House and the prayer breakfast movement in Washington, D.C. Because of his concern for this city and the needs of its people (70 percent of whom are black), he has spent much time with the inmates of nearby Lorton Prison, a maximum security facility with a reputation for outbreaks of violence and brutality. There, as a man of God, John moves among the men—getting to know them, loving them and thus earning the right to share his faith with them. Then he sticks with them through the long process of rehabilitation. Many lives have had new beginnings because John Staggers lets the love of Jesus flow through him to those who are behind bars. John is willing to lay down his life to help people in real trouble.

One young man we know in Washington, D.C., is a fruit of John's ministry at Lorton. Once a drug addict and a convict, he became a Christian while in prison. He's out on parole now, holding a responsible job and touching other lives for the Lord by his powerful testimony which is communicated not just by his words but by the life of love and caring he exhibits.

We also are involved with John in an urban task force here in the city, sharing our dream of Washington as a "city on a hill—for God." When task force members hear of a need, we have learned not to just rush out impulsively. We pray first. The theory, proven in practice, is that the real ministry comes out of love for the Lord and fellowship with one another as we abide in Jesus the Vine. It's easy to get all steamed up about a project, forgetting that unless it is approached prayerfully, the Spirit will be absent and then, too, the fruit.

One day the urban team heard about some elderly people who were living in an old house in the District. The house was in very poor condition—walls grimy, windows broken, the stench of human excrement throughout. It was winter and its occupants were nearly freezing to death with only a few blankets for the almost 50 people who lived there, as the icy wind swooped through every room.

After fellowship and prayer, a team went down to the house to deliver blankets, repair windows, clean bathrooms, and paint walls. But the ministry didn't stop there; a continuing relationship was established. Betty and Judy, two abiders as well as suburban housewives with backgrounds as social workers, continued to make themselves available. Knowing how to work with the agencies that can help people help themselves, these women poured out their lives for these people. They showed God's love in patience, kindness, gentleness—every fruit of the Spirit— as they waited in Social Security offices for hours, contacted AA counselors for alcoholics, found permanent housing for some, arranged hospitalization for others. Spirit-filled vessels, they ministered in the most practical ways even while they prayed.

The fruit of the Spirit—love, joy, peace, patience, kindness, goodness, faithfulness, gentleness, self-control—were all expressed in Mother Teresa's work. All were part of the local Washington ministries. It is impossible for people like Mother Teresa, John Staggers, Betty and Judy to abide in Him without bearing fruit.

I have not always known that. I think of the times in my life when as a new branch I was disappointed if I did not bear the specific kind of fruit I envisioned as right— disappointment in myself as though the responsibility of fruit-bearing was totally mine. I remember the sense of failure I felt when Mel, a person I befriended, cared for, prayed for and shared Christ with over a long period of time, failed to respond spiritually in any way apparent to me. I was crushed.

And then as I journeyed on, someone crossed my path and taught me this simple truth: *My* responsibility was to live a connected life (the branch to the Vine). The responsibility for the fruit was God's (the Vinedresser's). What a burden that lifted from me. A burden far too heavy for the branch of my life to bear, and besides, one that God had never designed it to carry. This is what Jesus meant when He said, "Apart from Me you can do nothing."

The more I immerse myself in this passage about fruit bearing, the more living examples I see all around me. There are Bill and Annette Anthony, a young couple in our congregation who have borne the fruit of peace in the midst of a trying situation.

Before their marriage Bill had been moving up in the business world very rapidly, with one promotion after another in a series of excellent jobs with top companies. At a young age he was put in charge of a 60-man accounting and data-processing department on a billion-and-a-half-dollar project. Gradually, the increased responsibilities and good fortunes began to build overconfidence and pride into Bill's life. These changes were so gradual and subtle, though, that Bill had not noticed any real difference in his style of life. But let Bill tell his own story.

While I cared about people on my staff and helped several in their careers, underneath it all my primary goal was advancing my own career. I had no thought that God might have a different plan for my life. Yet with each new job plateau, with each new material gain, there was an emptiness. Every new purchase became just a "toy," giving only short-lived satisfaction.

When Annette and I met, too much of my time was spent going through the motions of the Christian religion without really having a relationship with Christ and certainly not understanding the power of the Holy Spirit. But Annette and I were able to study the Bible together, and her commitment to the Lord helped me see a new dimension of Christianity.

I prayed that the Lord would forgive me for having accepted Him as a youth and then drifting so far away. Then one night I recommitted my life to Christ and asked Him to reveal Himself to me and to show me the power of the Holy Spirit.

The Lord must have been preparing me because a few months later I was called in by the controller of my company and fired. Naturally I was shaken, but somehow there was a peace within me and a joy I couldn't explain. I thanked the guy for firing me and tried to assure him that my life would be made better because of it. We had a terrific conversation and communicated better than we had in some time.

At that point Annette and I had been married about six months, and she was pregnant. When she came home from her job that day, I told her that I was out of a job. She accepted it remarkably well.

I took what I thought were logical steps. I put our house on the market and arranged our finances in order to last as long as possible. Annette was working, and I started collecting unemployment while looking for another job.

Meanwhile there was a lot of catching up for me to do as a Christian. Eager to learn more about the Lord, I often scheduled interviews to fit around my Bible studies. I started memorizing Scripture and praying a lot. Many days I spent hours at home reading the Bible, praising the Lord and singing along with albums I put on the stereo. These were joyous times.

The house sold and we moved into a tiny apartment a week before Annette went into the hospital to have our baby. By now we were both unemployed, and my unemployment checks had run out. It was the first time we'd really had to trust God for everything—rent, utilities, hospital bills and all!

Annette and I discussed whether or not she should file for unemployment, but this seemed wrong, since we both knew she would not be going back to work. "If we really trust the Lord," we said, "we won't need to do anything deceptive. We can just hang in there and know He's going to provide all we need."

Sure enough, He provided. A few weeks later I had a fine job offer I could not turn down from the U.S. Chamber of Commerce.

I asked Annette about her attitudes during this time of uncertainty. She just glowed. "We felt honored," she said, "to think that God loved us enough to give us the opportunity to have to trust Him completely. At first, we didn't have any idea the testing was going to be over such a long period, but every time a prospect fell through for Bill—and dozens of them did—we'd say, 'Lord, Your timing is perfect. You're going to give Bill the right job at just the right time.' We just refused to worry about it. What have I learned from all this? That God gives us peace and strength when we look to Him."

God not only gave peace and strength to Bill and Annette but also to many others who saw this fruit of the Spirit so beautifully manifested in their lives. And the fruit they bore also brought forth fruit in others who were struggling to trust God for personal needs. It has been a never-ending circle of blessing.

E. Stanley Jones once said that people can tell more about our faith from the way we *react* than the way we *act*. When life gives us a situation, our reaction tells much about who we are and whose we are. When our attitudes in adverse situations honor God, they are fruit that glorifies Him powerfully.

Some people bear rich fruit for their Lord by the sweet spirit of kindness and self-control they communicate in the midst of their affliction. One such woman was Ruth White, an invalid whose fruit was necessarily in being the Lord's person rather than in doing anything outwardly. When people came to visit her, they were invariably comforted by the love and joy of her life. She ministered to them even during the illness that ultimately took her life.

Some time after Ruth's death, her husband, Ken, married my friend, Harriet, another radiant Christian woman. One day Harriet confided, "Ruth must have been a marvelous mother—her children have all grown up to be beautiful people. She was in bed all those years, but just think what she was able to accomplish!" Ruth's attitude—an attitude filled with the real fruit of the Spirit—permeated the lives of her children. Her husband and his new wife honor her name and memory because her life honored and glorified God.

So it's not just in what we do that we honor God but in our loving, up-beat attitudes as well. The effectiveness of our inner life with God is often manifested in our genuine care for others. One mystic says it this way:

"Contemplation, at its highest intensity, becomes a reservoir of spiritual vitality that pours itself out in the most telling social action . . . Action is the stream, and contemplation is the spring. The spring remains more important than the stream, for the only thing that really matters is for love to spring up inexhaustibly from the infinite abyss of Christ and of God."

Yet, as Mother Teresa's life illustrates, our action is important: the spring has to flow freely or it will stagnate. Thomas Merton also says, "My soul does not find itself unless it acts. So it must act." The prophet Isaiah had this concern. After cataloging his nation's sins, and so revealing the reasons God was not receiving their worship or hearing their prayers, Isaiah outlined the avenues of restitution: ". . . learn to do good; seek justice, correct oppression; defend the fatherless, plead for the widow" (Isaiah 1:17).

If the people would do these things, the prophet said, then God would forgive them and restore blessing to the land.

Lord, were You saying that our praise and worship mean little

to You if we are not living out our faith in the arena of everyday
activity where it will count for somebody?

People who get excited about their walk with Jesus are
often criticized as being emotional, too caught up in feelings or too spiritual to be of any earthly good. But I am
finding more and more that these are the very people who
respond concretely to the needs of others with real help.
Instead of being indifferent to injustice or race relations,
they are often the first ones I see doing something about
social concerns as a result of their faith.

I know two elderly women, real abiders who choose
to do good and disappear. Inheritors of a substantial sum
of money, they regard it as a trust from God and use it
to give financial support to persons who are equipping
themselves to bear more fruit. We know one minister they
put through graduate school, and there are many others.

In California there is a couple who bore similar fruit
by making it a practice to live on 10 percent of what the
Lord supplied so they could give the other 90 percent away.
When Louie was starting a new mission church in Bel
Air, California, this couple came quietly to our rescue with
financial aid. Time and again over the years we met others
who had made it through difficult times because of their
generosity.

There is no way of measuring how many have been
helped through the years by the stewardship of these two
people. Always the help came without their being asked—
they just seemed to know. It came with no strings attached,
no repayment desired or permitted. Such generosity is a
fruit of the Spirit that helps others become fruit-bearers
too.

Not many of us have great financial wealth to share,
but we all have the talents God has given us. Archie and
Huldah Fletcher, a gifted surgeon and a nurse, for 28 years
have been pouring their life energy into the people of
Miraj, India. Our son, Tim, lived with the Fletchers while
he was a Volunteer in Mission working in the leper hospi-

tal. As part of their adopted family, Tim observed at close range the fruit that came as a result of their faithful, abiding lives.

But not many of us will be called to foreign soil. God uses everything we bring to Him at any time or place in our lives. Before his retirement, Bill Hill had been an editor of the *Washington Star*. Not exactly a rough and tough newspaper guy, Bill was nonetheless a yeasty journalist, far from the church. In being brought to church a few years ago by his wife-to-be Louise, he pleased his sister, Julia, as well—a lifelong believer who had been praying for her younger brother from the moment he was born.

Hearing the message of God for the first time—or at least the first time it had made any claim on his adult life—Bill was hooked. He came back Sunday after Sunday and finally gave his life to Christ. Today Bill is a real influence for the Lord in most everything that goes on at the church. To Louie, he's an answer to years of prayer for the right person to edit his sermons. To look at Bill now is to know that Christ is truly the crowning glory of his life. And when he talks about the Lord, his blue eyes fill with tears. He is yielding sweet, mellow fruit picked late from the branch of his life.

Another late fruit-producer is Dr. Lee Travis, sometimes called "the father of American speech pathology." A renowned psychologist and therapist, Dr. Travis was an agnostic when our first congregation began the construction of a church building in the hills directly above his home in Bel Air. When the workers were dynamiting for the building, Dr. Travis' house would shake, and the water in his swimming pool would splash around. He became more and more perturbed until one day, after the church was completed, he said to his wife, Lysa, "Well, I'm glad that monument to superstition is finally finished. Now maybe we can have some peace and quiet around here."

Later, watching the people make their way to the little church Sunday after Sunday, Dr. Travis grudgingly said

to his lovely Lysa, "Maybe we should go at least once to
see what's going on up there." They came to church together, not just once, but three Sundays in a row, and
in a deeply mystical, personal experience, Lee Travis encountered the living Christ.

Not long afterward, Louie and others were asked for
suggestions as to who might head a new graduate school
of Psychology at Fuller Theological Seminary. The name
of this new Christian with the impressive credentials was
mentioned again and again. And so in due course, Dr.
Lee Travis became the founding dean of the new school
of Psychology at Fuller Theological Seminary. Still an in-
credibly active and creative man, Dr. Travis continues to
bear delicious fruit for God.

When Lee Travis first had this experience that set his
life on a new path I remember thinking, *Lord, why didn't
this happen 30 years ago? More of his life could have been given
to You.* But even as I asked the question, I saw that something special had happened during the long waiting for
the harvest. His vast personal and professional experience
in the secular world gave him a profound understanding
of the problems of those caught up in the secular approach
to life. Late fruit, yes, but the years on the vine before
the harvest were hardly wasted!

People sometimes wonder at the zestful enthusiasm ex-
hibited by those whose gifts are harvested late. God ex-
plains, speaking through the prophet Joel: ". . . I will
restore to you the years that the locust hath eaten . . ."
(Joel 2:25). In a figurative sense, perhaps that means that
God will make up for our unproductive years with remarkable productivity. He has clearly done it with some of
the people we have come to know since we ourselves began
to abide in Him.

Dee and Bill Brehm are special covenant friends of ours.
They live beautiful, ordered lives and with their two child-
ren away at college, their home is very quiet. Dee and
Bill are knowledgeable about many areas of life where

we are novices, and one area is gourmet foods and wines. From their rich reservoir of knowledge Bill recently shared with us a fascinating story about the special sweetness of late fruit on a grapevine.

It seems that many years ago in the Rheingau district of Germany, when most of the vineyards were still church property cultivated by monks, the official consent of the bishop of the town of Fulda was required each year before the grape harvest could begin in that locality. In the latter half of the 18th century, when his grapes were ripe one fall, a vineyard master dispatched a messenger to the bishop at Fulda to gain his permission to begin the harvest. On the way, the messenger was set upon by robbers and did not return. Two weeks went by. The grapes were becoming overripe, starting to wizen on the branch, so a second messenger set out for Fulda. He, too, disappeared. Finally, as the vineyard master's beloved grapes were becoming more and more gray with mold and withered almost like raisins, the despairing monk sent a third messenger. He, at last, reached the bishop and brought back his authorization to begin the harvest.

Convinced that his whole crop was a failure, the monk decided to salvage what he could. He sent his pickers into the vines to collect the withered grapes which had only a little drop or two of juice remaining in them. With great trepidation the wine was made and put into casks for the beginning of the aging process. Then, in the early spring, when the wine was subjected to its first testing, it seemed a miracle had happened. To the great astonishment of those present, the wine turned out to be the best they had ever made! It was extremely mellow and sweet but with a natural sweetness, not cloying and obviously not man-made.

The wine made from the molded, withered grapes was so good that it revolutionized the industry in that part of the world. Even today some vineyard masters gamble against the appearance of a sudden frost in order to allow some of their grapes to remain on the vine and develop even further. Later, the grape pickers go into the vineyard and look for bunches of grapes that have been particularly affected by the "noble mold." They pick the grapes one by one, and the result is an extremely rare and expensive wine.

I thought again of my friends—Bill Hill, Lee Travis and others, and said, "Ah, yes, rare wine indeed."

Looking at what I considered to be fruit in my own life, I asked myself: Is it fruit that glorifies God? Is it fruit that demonstrates His love? I saw that any so-called fruit that pleased me but did not bring anyone closer to Him was wasted in God's eyes.

To feed the hungry—without love—would not show God to them. To do any other good thing without the love that comes from God would be useless to the Vinedresser.

What a touchstone He has given us for our decisions in life—for the choices we make, and the priorities we set: Will my doing this thing or that be only for show? Will it honor me? Or is this an opportunity to demonstrate the love of Jesus in a way that will make a lasting difference to somebody else?

If you abide in Me, and My words abide in you, ask whatever you will, and it shall be done for you.

The Storehouse

As long as I am abiding in Him and letting His words abide in me, the promise is that my prayers will be answered. Jesus repeats this promise several times in His teaching. ". . . whatever you ask in prayer, believe that you have received it, and it will be yours" (Mark 11:24). "Ask, and it will be given you; seek and you will find; knock and it will be opened to you" (Matthew 7:7).

So many promises! They suggest that God will fill our storehouse with His riches. But for now I am focusing on the one promise that my prayers would be answered if I would abide in Jesus and let His words abide in me. I had already pondered deeply what it meant for me to abide in Jesus; now I dwelled on what the other words meant—"if . . . My words abide in you."

If His words were abiding in me, I decided, they wouldn't be just sitting there; I would take them seriously, letting them be active in my life.

Years ago, an actress friend of mine told me about a dream she'd had. As I recall the scene, she was looking into a room crowded with people, all of them distraught— moaning, sobbing, wringing their hands. And in the way of dreams, she knew without being told that the reason for their distress was that they had lived and died feeling they'd missed the mark.

Suddenly the door of the room was opened and in walked the Person of Jesus Christ Himself. Seeing all the people in such distress, He was moved with compassion and began walking around the room, standing in front of each person in turn.

"My child, why are you crying?" He asked. "What can I do for you?"

"I'm crying, Lord, because my husband died when we were so young, and from then on, I was just lost without him. I wanted to serve You, but I've been lonely—too upset all these years to do anything."

"Oh, you didn't get My letter?" His voice was heavy with concern.

"What letter? Lord, did You write me a letter?"

"Oh, yes," He said. "I wrote and told you not to worry, that I would be closer to you than breathing and nearer than hands and feet. I told you that I would take the place of that missing one, that I would fill your life with meaning."

The woman looked surprised. "You know," she said, "the minister read that letter at my husband's funeral— but I didn't know it was *personal*—from You to me. If I had only known . . ."

Jesus stepped to the next person in the room, His head bowed with grief.

"Lord, I was poor all my life," that person told Him. "I couldn't live for You because I was too busy worrying about how I was going to put the next meal on the table, and . . ."

"Oh, then you didn't get My letter either?"

"No, Lord. Did You write me a letter?"

"Yes, My son. And in it I told you about the birds of the air—they don't worry about their next meal and yet they are fed. I told you to put Me first, for I had work for you to do, and I'd give you everything you really needed."

"Oh, Lord, I remember reading about that, but I didn't know You meant it for me!"

All around the room He went, and for every malady that was represented there were words of healing and help from Scripture. But no one had taken His words to heart. No one had His words actively abiding within.

I am not a student of dreams, and yet through the years I've thought of this story often and have been grateful to my friend for sharing its truth with me. In order to experience the best God has for me, I have to be like a little child—not childish but childlike—taking His words at face value and acting upon them.

There was a day (I'm jumping back several years now), when instead of sinking back into the welcoming softness of my special chair, I anxiously perched on its edge. There wasn't any major crisis in my life—but there were small things, almost-anxieties, pricking at me. I couldn't get my mind on the scripture passage I wanted to read that day because of another one that kept thundering through my mind: "Be anxious for nothing. Be anxious for nothing." It was clamoring to be noticed—to be obeyed.

I had to admit I was a little bit anxious—about everybody in the family. *That is ridiculous,* I told myself. They were all right as far as I knew; but still there was the gnawing uncomfortableness in me.

For one thing, the weather was ominous. When Louie had left two hours earlier in a single-engine Beechcraft with some of his covenant brothers to attend a meeting in Chicago, the morning sky had been bright and clear, the weather report good. *But what about those dark clouds I see now, Lord, and that whistling wind that's banging the loose shutter open and closed?*

"I know Louie is Yours," I said. "Please take care of

him and keep me from being anxious about him." In a little while, I was picturing the plane at 10,000 feet, the sun dancing on the clouds below him while Louie and his buddies sang together, loving every minute of their trip.

Then there was Dan at school in Santa Barbara, 3,000 miles from home, driving through freeway traffic, planning to go cross-country in his two-cylinder car when school was out. I knew he could handle himself. Dan was so steady, so responsible, and yet . . .

"Lord, I know Dan's where You want him to be right now. Make it all right with me too. I put him back in Your hands."

Why, Dan loved his "green aphid," as he called it—and he liked the thought of conserving energy with his 50-miles-per-gallon Honda. I released Dan from my anxious mind.

Tim was clear around the world working at the leper hospital at the Presbyterian Mission Station in Miraj, India. We knew there were painful inner struggles as he confronted the poverty and desperate need around him every day. *And Lord, I read somewhere that—though it's unlikely—leprosy can be contagious over a period of time.* I quickly shoved that picture out of my mind.

"Lord, let me think of the things of *good* report. Use this experience in Tim's life. And take away any useless anxiety I might have about it."

Andie was away from home for the first time. She had said she was loving the small, friendly campus of the College of Wooster in Ohio, yet hadn't I detected a tinge of homesickness in her voice the last time she'd called? "But Lord, I do trust Andie to Your care, too. Thank You for being with her and use everything she is experiencing to better fit her to be Your servant."

Jamie? Well, at least he'd be home when high school football practice was over for the day. I felt a wave of gratitude as I thought of answers to prayer we have had with our youngest. As a small boy Jamie was discovered to be dyslexic.

"Mommy, why can't I read like other children?" he asked.

"Daddy, am I dumb?"

Our hearts ached, as the hearts of parents the world over do when they sense one of their own has a struggle ahead with something that could affect the course of their lives. Believe me, we began to pray in earnest! Looking back, we thank God for an able doctor who diagnosed this accurately and prescribed wisely—prolonged and specialized retraining, daily reading at home and small classroom learning situations at school with firm yet understanding teachers.

Our small son learned that dyslexia was not his fault, not something "wrong," but something "different," something he could overcome if he would work very hard.

Jamie accepted the challenge, and God has graciously answered our prayers, I believe, by giving him a discipline and tenacity that has amazed us all these years—a discipline that will serve him well in whatever task God calls him.

Thank You, Lord, for helping Jamie in his struggle. And please, God, help the many children who even now are wrestling with the distraction of dyslexia. And then help me to keep my hands (and my anxious mind) off what doesn't belong to me—like other people's lives.

I remembered a passage I had read just a few days earlier in *Letters and Papers from Prison* by Dietrich Bonhoeffer. I found it easily as the book fell open to the page with the turned-down corner. Again it spoke to me:

"From the moment we awake, until we fall asleep, we must commend our loved ones wholly and unreservedly to God, and leave them in His hands, transforming our anxiety for them into prayers on their behalf."

Before I had finished the prayers for our family, I was leaning back and relaxing in the chair, ready to listen and no longer harboring anxious thoughts. How good it was to know Him—and to experience His faithfulness in answering prayer. It was a faithfulness He demonstrated every time I was faithful to ask and take Him at His word. That reminded me again of Henrietta Mears, our "Teacher" in the College Department at the Hollywood Presbyterian Church. Shortly before she died, she was asked if there was anything she would change if she had her life to live over. That powerful woman of God said simply, "Yes, I would believe God more."

Asking and believing come hard sometimes, but Jesus' command to us is especially penetrating in the original text, as translated by Kenneth S. Wuest: "If you maintain a living communion with Me and My words are at home in you, I command you to ask, at once, something for yourself, whatever your heart desires, and it will become yours."

But wait! That sounds selfish, almost dangerous to ask "something for myself." How can I be sure that what I would ask would be in line with what God wants for me? Yet, if I am abiding—living and growing in Him—and if His words are alive and real in my life—then couldn't the desires I have be those implanted by the Vinedresser Himself? Yes, we need to ask and receive, trusting that He is molding our desires; and we will bear fruit for Him.

Then I reread John 15:7–8, this time in my New International Version of the Bible. I saw something I'd never seen before. Its wording went like this: "If you remain in Me and My words remain in you, ask whatever you wish, and it will be given you. This is to My Father's glory . . ." The verse goes on to talk about the fruit we bear and about our being His disciples, both of which certainly bring Him glory. Yet suddenly I wondered if the word "this" could also refer to the preceding verse. Our asking and His answers must also bring glory to the Father. What a revelation that was. And although my commentaries made no mention of this, I found plenty of confirmation in my own heart.

Sometimes, I knew, those who observed the fruit did not give the glory to God. They might make the mistake of praising the fruit instead of the Vine whose power produced it. Or they might praise the branch through which the fruit came instead of praising the Vine that made it possible. But whenever the fruit bearers give witness to their need and how they have turned to God, who then supplied above all they could ask or think, then it is God indeed who is glorified and honored.

No wonder it's important to Him that we ask, and then receive. That insight put me in a frame of mind to ask for more—not for my own selfish indulgence but that my fruit for God and others might be increased, and that His name might be honored.

As I sat in the rocking chair remembering the day when the Lord had calmed my mild uneasiness about the family, He brought poignantly to my mind the night when I had asked for and received His peace in the midst of a most painful time of my life. It had to do with my mother.

Mom. I thought of how she had looked when I was growing up—dark hair, beautiful hazel eyes, pretty skin, shapely legs. To me, she was wonderful in every way.

Mother always had to work hard. It must have been difficult, even in those days, to support us both on a salary of $25 a week working in the office of an insurance firm. But she somehow managed and provided a secure, simple home for the two of us even during the years we lived with my grandfather and especially after his death.

My friends loved her. In my teen years, hordes of young people descended on our house, because as they said, "Your mom is someone we can talk to about our problems. She listens and understands—never puts us down." They all called her by her first name, Stella, and they included her in their fun as if she was one of them.

And yet, for all her fun-loving, Mother had the true wisdom to let people live their own lives. Even me. The love she had wasn't a "smother love." For instance, when

I came home from the conference where I had experienced a mature encounter and yielding of my life to Christ, I naturally told her all about it. She didn't say much—she never did. But I can still see her hearing me out, her lovely eyes filling with tears; I knew she understood. Because her own church background had been narrow and legalistic and had once threatened to quench her young spirit, she was a bit afraid at first that my "religious experience" would take the joy out of life for me. But she soon found that committing my life to Christ had opened wonderful new dimensions for me, and eventually she too embraced the Lord in a more open and deeper way.

Some time later I left my career with the motion picture industry because I recognized that God had another direction for me. Some of the people I was close to were actually angry at me, almost trying to live my life for me. But Mom? She was right with me, wonderfully supportive as always. Her attitude: "If this is the right thing for you, I'm all for it."

Mother had a nonpossessive, hands-off kind of love that showed me she was never interested in how my achievements might build her up, but always and only her heart's concern was what was best for me.

After I was married and she became a grandmother, all our children adored her. They loved her visits. When one of them would come in from a party or date, Mom would invite them to share their good times with her. There was never any anxious probing, just a joyful, lighthearted, "Come on, kiddo, tell me all about it." Mom was never demonstrative or mushy, but she had an affirming, fun-loving spirit we all adored. "Mimi" was what our kids called her, and it was a mutual admiration society from the beginning.

All these memories came flooding to my mind one night just over a year ago when Louie and I were wakened from a deep sleep by the ringing of the telephone. I jumped out of bed and reached for the phone on my desk.

A long-distance call for me. My stepfather, Jim Wilhelm, the precious man to whom my mother had been happily married for 30 years, was calling from California. His voice was full of anguish.

"Oh, my God, I can't believe it. My Stella's gone—your mother's dead . . ."

Mom gone? She couldn't be! I had talked to her just yesterday. I knew she'd not been feeling too well and was in the hospital for tests. But gone? No, God, no!

Even at that moment, my suitcase sat half-packed in our room. Louie and I had planned to fly out in a few days so the four of us—Mother, Jim, Louie and I—could take a trip together, ending in Santa Barbara for our son Dan's graduation the following week. How Mom had looked forward to that—the first grandson's graduation from college. But now . . . no, I couldn't believe it. And yet it was terribly true.

"Heart attack," he said.

I felt a cold mass in my chest, and I began to tremble uncontrollably. I heard words coming from my mouth:

"Oh, Grampa. Just hold on. I'll be there with you as soon as I can get a flight out."

I was aware of his awful need and wanted to comfort him, but my own pain and loss were overwhelming me.

Louie went downstairs to heat some milk for a warm drink, and I fell to my knees beside our bed. Waves of sorrow washed over me as I thought of the woman who had been both mother and father to me as I grew up, the person who so committed herself to me that I always felt secure in her love and safe in the home she worked so hard to maintain. She had always been such a pal, so much fun to be with—a terrific mother. Even after my marriage, though miles and long stretches of time separated us, we remained close.

I ached to hold her in my arms or walk with her hand in mine as we had always done when we were together. My sorrow was too deep for tears. Everything in me cried out, "Oh, God, help! I can't make it unless You help me."

I hardly knew what to ask Him for; I could only abandon myself to Him, looking to His strength to fill my weakness.

As I knelt there calling, crying out to God, I was aware of a change gently coming over me, a warm blanket of love enveloping me. I felt His strength absorbing my weakness, and suddenly I knew that not only would I make it but there would be strength to share with others.

Jamie was the first to need it. He came in from a date soon after Louie came up from the kitchen. We called him into our room and as he sat on the edge of our bed we told him what had happened. Like me, he couldn't believe it at first.

"Oh no, not Mimi," he protested, almost confidently. "It couldn't be Mimi. Why it seems it was just the other day that we were saying good-by in front of their house in California. She stood there on the sidewalk by our car and kind of danced a jig. I can still hear her teasing and laughing while she did it, saying 'How's that for an old girl?' I just can't believe that Mimi's . . ."

Jamie's voice broke then. He did believe it. And as we asked, the Holy Spirit came to comfort him too. To make him glad for all the happy memories, all the fun and love he'd shared with Mimi.

On the flight to California, the much needed tears began to flow. Even in the midst of them, I marveled that my heart could hurt so much, and yet I could feel such all-pervading peace. When Louie's mother and father met me at the airport, I could tell they'd been praying for my strengthening too. Louie's father, so dignified and noble; Louie's mother, so appreciative of everything, always seeing the good in things, her thankfulness made me thankful. Just seeing them, so beautiful and right together, triggered deep feelings of love and gratitude for them—and such a deep sense of loss for my own mother—that the tears streamed down again. But even as they drove me to be with my stepfather and his daughter, Gloria, the infusion of God's strength and that remarkable peace was still with me.

The powerful Presence was with me in a real way in the days and events that followed, too. Choosing a coffin, clothes for Mother to wear, making arrangements for the memorial service, greeting people, going through her things afterward—painfully poignant reminders of the life we'd shared.

I was immeasurably stronger than my usual self, and I knew it was because I was relying utterly on my God. There was no way I could make it without Him. I knew it—and He knew it. Leaning on Him every moment, asking and receiving what He gave, I experienced His power and peace as a fruit of His Spirit in me. Such peace I could never have known if I had not abandoned myself to His care. He really does fill our storehouse with his riches.

But how important it is to ask—so that we might receive.

Lord, without Your grace, Your strength to replace my weakness when Mother went to be with You, I simply couldn't have made it. Thank You, Lord, that You didn't leave me on my own. Lord, teach me to be dependent on You in the ordinary days too—that my life might be a witness to what You can do.

These things I have spoken to you,
that My joy may be in you, and that
your joy may be full.

Joy from the Vine

The above promise of Jesus could not be clearer—if we abide in Him and He in us, we will live in the fullness of His joy, a joy that is overflowing! Whenever I have not accepted that joy and appropriated it into my life, I have cheated myself and others.

Some years ago I wrote a book about joy, but I keep discovering new things about it. One is that the joy Jesus gives to abiders is absolutely independent of circumstances, a joy that is the direct result of the Vine Life.

If Jesus is abiding in my life, and I am abiding in Him, there is no way I can fail to be joyful. It was in the upper room, as His darkest hour approached, that Jesus said, "These things have I spoken . . . that My joy may be in you . . . that your joy may be full." And so in our dark hours and the upper rooms of our lives, His joy—far better, far deeper than mere happiness—can be abundantly ours. Joy is proof that—His life in us is real.

It is so very important for us to see joy for what it is: a result of a relationship with God, and not something dependent on life's circumstances. Christians are not immune from unhappy events and pain. Suffering is a stubborn fact of life. No one escapes. The joy of Christ is there in the midst of—and in spite of—life's pain.

Within the last month a couple we know have experienced the loss of their college-aged daughter in a sudden, totally unexpected death. A card just received from them speaks eloquently:

"She is gone from us, but she had given her heart to Christ and is with Him now. Thank God . . . but we miss her desperately! Someday we will understand, but for now we are claiming the promise in 2 Corinthians: 'Blessed be God . . . who comforteth us in all our tribulation, that we may be able to comfort them which are in any trouble, by the comfort wherewith we ourselves are comforted of God.' The Bible never says life will be easy. Grief is real, but we can have joy in Jesus even when our hearts are breaking."

Another friend experienced a similar kind of joy and peace in the midst of disaster. Her son was in a terrible automobile accident, and he hung between life and death for many days. As she traveled back and forth to the hospital day and night, she could have been caught up in awful agony. But people were praying—and the prayers were getting through. One day when her son was still hovering near death, my friend told me, "You know, there has to be some reason for this peace that I feel—and even joy!" She went on to explain that she knew most people wouldn't understand joy in the midst of such circumstances, but she knew she was being lifted by the prayers of God's people and by His Spirit in her life. Whether her son lived or died could not alter this. It turned out that he lived.

But can that kind of joy last? I asked myself. What happens when the crisis is over and the friends go back to their daily routines and forget to keep her lifted up? And then I remembered our good friends, Jim and Margaret Milner. Here is their story in their own words.

It happened on a beautiful Indian summer Saturday in September, 1965. Our Jimmy was a 17-year-old senior in high school, vitally interested in sports, people and in a church youth group. The weekend was a special retreat for the group at a camp near Annapolis, Maryland, with vivacious, talented young seminary leaders, Bob and Hazel Terhune, in charge. Margaret and I had gone for a picnic in nearby Great Falls, Virginia. We'd had a wonderful day and hoped Jimmy and his group were having one too. We got home about 10 o'clock that night and hadn't been in the house more than five minutes when the doorbell rang. Margaret opened it.

Bob Terhune was standing on the porch with one of our best friends. Even in the dim glow of the porch light, I could see that their faces were ashen. Margaret saw it too.

"Where's Jimmy?" my wife asked, the color draining from her face as she tried to push her way past them. Gently they led her to the couch, and when we were both seated, they told us, in halting, broken sentences that there'd been an accident at the camp. The group had gone swimming at four o'clock, they said, during a scheduled recreation period. Jimmy had dived in with the rest of them, but . . .

In all the happy splashing, no one noticed that he hadn't come back to the top of the pool. If they had noticed it, they'd have assumed he was swimming under water, which he loved to do. Moments later they discovered him lying on the bottom. They'd tried artificial respiration for a long time but with no success.

We were in shock, drowning ourselves in grief, sinking down, down, down—unable to grasp what had happened. Staggering, overwhelming, piercing pain penetrated every fiber of our beings. "Oh God, oh God, what is this all about? So young—we'll never see his quick smile, hear his bright call as he bangs through the door. No more—ever, ever, ever . . ."

The kind, loving words of our friends could not penetrate the wall of numbness and shock.

"Lord, You promised never to leave us or forsake us. What

does this mean? We've claimed Your abiding promise so many times for others. How awkward, inadequate and insignificant *our* words always seemed—but You always came to their rescue. What we've only talked about before, we're experiencing for ourselves now. Help, Lord, help! Come to *our* rescue!

"Is this how You felt, Lord, when Your Son was on the cross? Is this what You gave because You loved us so much? It's unendurable, Lord!"

And then the Word of the Lord came, right in the midst of that awful darkness. From somewhere in the scriptures salted away in my memory I heard the words, "Enoch walked with God; and he was not, for God took him." Where was that? Genesis, of course (Genesis 5:24). But what it seemed to say right now was that Jimmy's death was so sudden he felt no pain, no struggle, just a sudden turning loose of life to be with His Lord.

"Yes, Lord, I'll believe that."

And then the flood of comfort, the awareness that there would be no more sinking down because we were upheld by the everlasting arms. *Let not your heart be troubled . . . I go to prepare a place for you . . . I will not leave you comfortless . . . I will come to you . . . If a man love me, he will keep My words . . . My Father will love him, and we will come and make our abode with him . . . The Comforter . . . Peace I leave you . . . that your joy might be full.*

Then our response to Him: "O dear Father; Jesus; Comforter—let us truly abide in You that others may be comforted with this same indescribable nearness and comfort as You reveal Yourself to us through these friends You have sent us. Thank You for the peace You've given us now, Lord. May Jimmy's life—even in death—be the Christian witness You would have it be, and may many come to know Your love through his life and ours."

Years have passed. We can and do still weep, particularly when we visit Jimmy's grave in Arlington Cemetery. But our tears are not grief—they're gratitude and joy for all He has accomplished.

The Milners have joy because He is in their lives. It is a sign of lives abiding in the Vine—for this kind of joy has no other source. So it is with a woman I know who

was told that her much-longed-for child, born severely
retarded and physically maimed, would never be a normal
little girl. And yet the mother witnesses bravely and genuinely to God's presence with her in the pain. She prays
for a miracle but accepts with quiet inner joy the surety
that in the life to come all things will be made new.

Malcolm Muggeridge entitled his book about Mother
Teresa *Something Beautiful for God.* In visiting her "Home
for the Dying" in Calcutta, India, he expected to be depressed by the people inside who had literally been picked
up off the streets. Yet his most memorable impression of
the place was joy because it was in so many faces.

This kind of tough joy can be a powerful influence on
those who are close enough to see that it is real. It can
also irritate those who might want it very much but not
knowing how it comes, choose to doubt and scoff instead.
Even in very normal, everyday living, there are those who
are downright uncomfortable with happy people.

A pastor with a Ph.D. in psychology who has served
with us in two churches had that infectious spirit. While
part of a small therapy group, he encountered a man who
seemed offended by his attitude.

"Can't you ever wipe that silly smile off your face?"
the man asked belligerently. "What are you so happy
about?"

Genially our friend countered with the question: "Why,
does it bother you?"

This was the opening wedge to an exchange which ena-
bled the unhappy man to reveal a number of frustrations.
And the pastor remained free to be himself and let his
joy show. Too often we back off through intimidation.

Albert Schweitzer said, "There's so much coldness in
the world because we are afraid to be as cordial as we
really are."

Joy is okay, the world seems to say, if we have some
excuse for it. Like when your favorite team wins or you
get a raise in pay or you sit down to your favorite meal.

If we have no obvious reason for our joy we're likely to be judged severely: "She always acts so happy, she makes me sick."

But we need to risk being different in order to express the joy of the Lord which is not dependent on anything that happens to us externally but on a great act that has happened to us internally. The Bible does not say joy is a fruit of circumstance; it states that joy is a fruit of the Spirit. Joy is the evidence of God in our lives. The question is, will we accept it? Will we be willing to be God's peculiar people, and like our friend, be free enough to ask, "Why does my joy bother you?" And if it does bother someone, can we conclude that this might be *his* problem? There should be no hiding a promised joy from God.

And this promised joy is found in unexpected places. I know it when I am smiled at by a somber old gentleman at church who rarely smiles or when the schedule slows enough to allow me time to play all day in my kitchen and cook a special dinner for friends. There is joy as we break bread together and take time to enjoy one another.

And there is health in being spontaneous in expressing these good feelings from God. Sometimes we need an occasional physical outlet for the overflow of joy in life. Have you ever felt that way? I have and I know I am not to stifle those feelings in the name of dignity. When life is full of meetings, conferences, work and people-problems that often defy solutions, it's important for me to establish a tiny corner labeled, "PURE FUN. NOTHING SERIOUS ALLOWED HERE."

Two years ago my friend Mary Jane challenged me to take tap-dancing lessons with her. I had no special desire to learn tap dancing and wondered how I could ever use the skill. When my friend said, "All my life I've wanted to tap dance, and I'm determined to learn before I'm 50," I agreed to go with her. I thought, *Why not?* I needed to exercise. And it would be fun.

The rest of the class was between the ages of 14 and

21, and there we were—middle-aged and looking utterly ridiculous, I'm sure. But what a joy it was, laughing at ourselves until our sides ached and feeling all the while the Lord was right there with us and joining with us in our laughter.

One Thursday night recently—the night Louie and I try to put aside for each other—we succumbed to the urge to do something special and different. Sometimes we go out for dinner for what we call our "quality time," but the budget said a loud "no" to that. What could we do that would be relaxing and not cost anything?

Across the street from our house is a large soccer field. It was covered with crisply beautiful autumn leaves, and the weather was so fine that Louie and I decided to go and walk among them. They felt so good on our feet that we made a huge mound of the fallen leaves, jumped into the midst of them and made ourselves a cozy nest. Lying there on our backs, we talked, laughed and watched the planes from nearby National Airport fly over. We had a special time of communication.

When people happened by, jogging or walking their dogs, we'd shout "Hello there!" and send them on their way, probably wondering, "What ails them?"

Well, we were just celebrating joy, enjoying a night out on the town.

"Except you become as a little child . . ." I need to be reminded of that truth, and spontaneity helps. If we let ourselves become pompous and full of the sense of our own importance—self-consciously dignified—I'm afraid Heaven will be quite a shock to us, for Heaven will be filled with joy. The here and now can be joyful as well— as we abide in Him.

Each of us can express the Spirit's joy in a unique and natural way. It does not require a bubbly personality or a perpetual smile. That would be rather much. But in the Vine Life there is an inner radiance that will shine through whatever God-given personality we have as evidence of the presence of Jesus in our lives.

This does not mean we will escape knowing depression, or never slip into a negative slump. Scripture is full of such examples among God's own people. Jeremiah was so depressed he cursed his own birth, yet he discovered hope in the way God dealt with His people. Job, the example of classic clinical depression, found joy again in the mystery that God is God, transcendent and powerful, able to change even the human heart. And in the New Testament, Peter, after his denial of Christ and subsequent feelings of worthlessness and guilt, was able to go through all that to the joy of experiencing Christ's forgiveness.

Scripture tells us that depression is real. But depression, to most of us, is bearable because we believe it will pass sooner or later. The "light at the end of the tunnel" is at least dimly seen. And by opening ourselves to God's love and light, the "Slough of Despond" can be faced.

But there are those times in the lives of even some of God's people when feelings plunge beyond depression to the level of despair. Despair is being trapped in that same tunnel but with no light visible at either end; it is when we look to our own devices for escape and find we have none that will help; it is when we feel as if God has shut us into "a place of smooth walls." As the prophet Jeremiah puts it: "He has dragged me into the underbrush and torn me with His claws, and left me bleeding and desolate. I have forgotten what enjoyment is. All hope is gone; my strength has turned to water, for the Lord has left me" (Lamentations 3:9, 11, 17, 18, TLB).

What about the Christian who is locked in this emotional prison—a predicament where there is no light, no escape?

If we were to leave it there, the only answer would be suicide: Why even bother to live under such circumstances? But Jeremiah did not leave it there and neither can we. If we read on we find one ray of hope.

"His compassion never ends. It is only the Lord's mercies that have kept us from complete destruction. Great is His faithfulness; His lovingkindness begins afresh each day . . . therefore I will hope in Him . . . It is good both to hope and wait quietly for [Him] . . ." (Lamentations 3:22–24, TLB).

For some, that is ultimately all there is to cling to. But I am convinced that although "weeping may tarry for the night . . . joy comes with the morning" (Psalm 30:5). Sometimes we just have to wait for the Lord to act. But His promise is certain: He *will* act.

My tap-dancing friend, who is by profession a pastoral counselor, says, "The mature Christian sees hope in depression and understands, bone-deep, that joy will come again because God is always caring and offering relationships anew."

Pope John Paul II has this inner joy. There is no other explanation for the way he plunges, grinning, into crowds, raising children high in the air, throwing his arms around old acquaintances and blessing the needy. *Time* magazine called it "an extraordinary, low-burning joy—joy in adversities endured, joy in the signs of national pride and faith that he saw before him, joy in being a Christian, in being human."

But why not? We read that the first Christians were literally called children of joy and that the "religious" art of the early followers of Jesus was very different from that with which we are so familiar today. The image of Jesus found in pictures in the catacombs, painted by refugees hiding for safety, is a joyous one. A biblical scholar, Dean Arthur Stanley, wrote, "Look at that beautiful, graceful figure, bounding down as if from his native hills, with the happy sheep nestling on his shoulder, with the pastoral pipes in his hand, blooming in immortal youth . . . strong, the joyous youth, of eternal growth, of immortal grace."

Jesus' joy bothered some of the people of His day. "Who is this man," they wanted to know, "who enjoys parties and weddings and all kinds of people? Who is this friend of publicans and sinners?" And He admitted it when He spoke freely of "My joy," and was always giving thanks for something.

Jesus saw life as good and was amazed, as He still must be today, at the number of people who found so little for which to be joyously grateful.

One of the most joyous persons I know is Louie's mother. As I write this our family is sharing two weeks in the mountains of California with Mother and Dad Evans, and I have been touched once again by the beauty and joy in her life. Every lovely vista we see, every special time of family sharing or worship, any kindness shown, even the daily weather—good or bad—is reason enough for a genuine expression of gratitude from Mother Evans.

The secret of the joy in this strong woman's life is easy to see. It is thankfulness. I wonder: If I were more faithful in expressing my thanksgiving for *all* things, would my joy be more full?

Those who, by choice, reject the faith are always watching the believers closely, evaluating our beliefs by the way we react to misfortune and upsets. When His joy shines through our heartache, He is able to touch the stony or despairing hearts of others. We can claim such joy as part of our Vine Life. It is impossible for us really to live in Jesus, as a branch in a vine, and not have His joy flowing into us.

In *A Severe Mercy*, Sheldon Vanauken expressed it this way: "The best argument for Christianity is Christians . . . their joy, their certainty, their completeness. But the strongest argument against Christianity is also Christians—when they are somber and joyless, when they are self-righteous and smug in complacent consecration, when they are narrow and repressive. Then Christianity dies a thousand deaths . . . but there are impressive indications that the positive quality of joy is in Christianity and possibly nowhere else."

Lord, prove Your joy in me!

Other Branches

As I reread the verse, I felt a twinge of conscience. If we're to love others as He loves us, that means we are to love without strings attached. We are also to love those who may hate us or hurt us. I have to confess I don't always love everybody with that kind of love.

There was Mr. Harper who seemed to have a special kind of hostility toward our family. People had warned us of this man when we first moved into the neighborhood. His house was on a hill nearby and had a long, steeply sloping backyard covered with ice plants to keep the top soil in place. Around his yard he had posted heavy iron chains. But nothing he did prevented the neighborhood children from racing down and across his long backyard.

"Mr. Harper has been a cranky old goat ever since I've known him," more than one neighbor told me. "Can't get along with anybody. No need for you to try, Coke, you'll just be beating your head against a stone wall."

I didn't believe them. The very warning was a challenge
to me. I thought I'd prove them wrong and really work
my way into Mr. Harper's heart. One of the first things
I did after we had moved and were settled was to bake a
fresh strawberry pie and take it to his front door. He did
look rather surly when he answered my knock, but he
accepted the pie with a curt, "Thank you." Then he
slammed the door in my face, not inviting me in.

"Oh, well," I thought out loud, "he's probably a bit
shy and my visit surprised him. When he gets used to
us it'll be different."

We made other overtures as a family. Sometimes when
I baked cookies, I'd send one of the children to his house
with a dozen still warm from the oven on a paper plate
(after he had failed to return my pie pan). There was usually a gruff acknowledgment, but he never invited any
one of us in, and he never initiated any contact of his
own until the Saturday he came absolutely storming to
our door late in the afternoon. Under his arm was a cardboard box and he literally pounded on our door until I
opened it. Without any preliminaries he thrust the box
at me.

"Look at them!" he shouted. "Look at them! Ice plants
from my yard. Ruined, shredded to pieces by the shenani-
gans of those rough-neck hooligans of yours. Riding down
my hill in cardboard boxes, they were. This afternoon.
Tore up the whole slope. It'll cost me a hundred dollars
to get it replanted. I oughta call the law!"

As he paused for breath I took a deep one myself, and
tried to speak calmly. "Hold on, Mr. Harper. I'm sorry
your plants are ruined. But my boys didn't do it. They've
been working in our garage all afternoon. Go and see for
yourself."

My words were polite enough, but the pent-up frustration of months of trying to be a good neighbor was near
the breaking point.

Mr. Harper didn't give me a chance to say anything

else. He just repeated his angry tirade as if he hadn't heard a word I'd said.

Oooh! That did it!

I don't remember much of the conversation from then on—only that my heart was pounding and my face was flushed. I was as angry as a she bear whose cubs had been attacked. I was also furious at this man for not allowing any of us into his life.

We jawed at each other. Then he turned and retreated down the walk, his shoulders slumped, fury spent—for the time being.

I tried to put Mr. Harper out of my mind, but I couldn't. The day after our explosion I sat in my rocker with a heavy spirit. In my prayer I confessed my frustration. "Lord, I've tried to love Mr. Harper and failed. He is impossible . . ."

I stopped, unable to continue. "None of My children is impossible." I could almost hear the Lord's words.

"But, Lord, I've tried. I really have." My tone had a touch of petulance. I was struggling, arguing—on the defensive.

There was deep silence. I had something else to confess, and I did so. "Lord, I lost my temper with Mr. Harper. Forgive me."

Just saying the words lightened my spirit. Not completely, of course. I still couldn't love the man.

Then came an understanding of myself. My vulnerable area was my family. There was too much sensitivity here—and pride. While I realized my husband and children had faults, I did not want others to point them out. Especially someone like Mr. Harper.

I admitted something else. My indignation over Mr. Harper's accusation was much overdone. The boys had not been guilty yesterday, but other days they had slid down Mr. Harper's sloped yard in boxes. I had heard them talking about how much fun it was.

What should I do about this, Lord?

Love Mr. Harper as I have loved you.

Ouch! So I tried a different approach with Mr. Harper. I tried to look at Mr. Harper as Jesus saw him—a lonely, wounded, scarred individual, alienated from the world which had probably hurt him cruelly. Jesus would have eyes of compassion. I could too. I could never love him on my own effort. But that wasn't necessary. Just as abiding is not something I can do on my own but is something the Lord does in me, so too would He love an unlovely person from this place in me. *I am the Vine, you are the branches.*

The experience with Mr. Harper helped me grow in several ways. I thought I could love just anyone on my own. Not so: only with God's help. And if I didn't let Him love the unlovely through me, I lost the sense of His peace and presence in my life.

We moved away from this neighborhood before I could tell if my new attitude toward Mr. Harper was making any difference in his life. But it was making a difference in mine.

Only after much prayer did Louie accept the call to National Presbyterian Church in Washington, D.C. Though it was difficult to leave California and the people we loved and the ocean we enjoyed, Washington has become my favorite city in all the world. I thrill to the history—the beautiful buildings, the outrageously lovely springs and the stimulating people from every race and background.

And I thrill especially to the many "salt-of-the-earth" people in the congregation with whom we have been called to serve.

Any minister in any church—anyone in leadership—expects some opposition from those whose perceptions and goals might differ; Louie expects it and so do I. But what I have been discovering again in myself here in Washington is that criticism of Louie is harder on me, I think, than on him.

To a great extent, I have been able to deal with it. Sometimes I'm even able to laugh about it and forget some of the hard spots. Our son, Dan, always honest and direct, says I own a "selective memory" that screens out the bad and remembers only the good. However, that isn't the whole story. The truth is I am still very tender indeed in regard to my family. Accuse my children unjustly as Mr. Harper did years ago, and you'll hear from me; hurt Louie, deal with him in a way I consider unfair, and I really feel it. I have finally come to grips with the fact that it matters far too much to me what others think of those I love. I have continued to struggle with the lesson Mr. Harper unknowingly taught me: that it must be God Himself loving those people through me, especially those who might tread in this area of my vulnerability. Some may say that this is a natural instinct of love. And up to a point I agree. But I know that at times I have crossed the line of love's instinct and become too protective. Then it is my pride which is injured most.

The bad news is that I'm still struggling; the good news is that the struggle is being resolved as God continues to work with me in this area of my life. And as I ask Him to nurture in me the capacity to bear such injuries, if need be, He puts within me the right attitude toward the people involved.

And so I come back to my relationship to Jesus. He is the Vine and I one of the branches. His power—the life-giving, vital sap—flowing through me enables me, in turn, to forgive and love others. As branches, we are all flawed. To pretend otherwise is to be untruthful and to refuse the healing flow of His power in our lives. The love of Jesus for us is overwhelming. He doesn't turn away from us no matter what we do, because we are connected. Nothing can separate us from His love, and that's how He wants our love to be for one another.

Andrew Murray experienced it: "Jesus will give you the divine love in your heart with which you can love people. That is the meaning of the assurance: 'The love of God is shed abroad in our hearts by the Holy Spirit . . .' Christ can give you a fountain of love, so that you cannot help loving the most wretched and the most ungrateful, or those who have wearied you hitherto . . ."

I am not to try to love those who hurt and weary me; Jesus will do that through me if I am willing to be a branch connected to Him as the Vine.

There is much we have to learn about the relationship of one branch to another. The natural vine thrives only when all parts are in health, in balance, in harmony, each submitted to the Vinedresser who cares for the whole vine in order to enable it to fulfill its potential of fruit production. The whole plant flourishes—and glorifies God—only when each part is in a healthy, integral relationship with the other parts. All parts must *work together* for the common good.

In a sense, this is what Jesus is saying in John 15:12: "Love one another; lay down your lives for one another as I have laid down My life for you."

How aware I am that Jesus did not love with lip service only; He went to the cross. The first letter of John says, "By this we know love, that He laid down His life for us; and we ought to lay down our lives for the brethren. But if any one has the world's goods and sees his brother in need, yet closes his heart against him, how does God's love abide in him? Little children, let us not love in word or speech but in deed and in truth" (1 John 3:16–18).

Recently a young man we know was in a tragic automobile accident. Formerly a tennis champion, now he was in the hospital with a broken neck, almost entirely paralyzed. Immediately his church youth group decided to "love in deed" and formed a 24-hour prayer chain to intercede for him. Every hour of the day and night, someone was praying. A prayer circle containing dozens of names was drawn on a large poster and hung on the wall of his hospital room so that he could look at it during any hour and know who was praying for him then.

Before long, there was a creeping, inch-by-inch response. First, he was able to move his thumbs, a toe—and then some feeling was restored to his arms. Admittedly, he has a long way to go, but a miracle of courage and perseverance has already been won in his life. Because of his attitude and the loving prayers of his friends the miracle continues day by day.

I have long been impressed that almost all the healings Jesus performed took place in the presence of other people—some who were perhaps only curious, but in many cases persons who were concerned and caring. Today I see the same thing: God heals most often in the company of a caring, loving community—people whose lives are centered in Christ, like branches relating to other branches.

How fulfilling it is to love one another simply by being in relationship—supporting and caring for one another in fellowship, bearing one another's burdens, sharing one another's joys and struggles, confessing and praying together. But to love in "deed and truth" will also involve action—and sacrifice on our part. As someone has put it, "We not only need 'born again' Christians—but 'sell all you have and give to the poor' Christians: people who take seriously what Jesus said to the rich young ruler as well as what was said to Nicodemus."

As Christians we all constitute the Body of Christ. Some are eyes or heart or brain. It's obvious what they do—preachers, counselors, evangelists, teachers, helpers. But some are tendons or ear lobes or mesentery or blood-vessel muscles—not as obvious but nevertheless needed for the whole body to work together smoothly. These parts must not be underestimated even though they might appear insignificant at first glance.

On the vine we see fruit and leaves. The hidden parts—roots, small tendrils, the conducting tissues within the vine, the sap, the chlorophyll molecules—all are vitally important. That they all work together is essential. It is one of the most profound ways to demonstrate our faith to the non-Christian world.

On the natural vine, one branch can overlap another and keep it from the life-giving sun. It is possible that a spiritual branch can do the same thing—interfere with a brother's relationship to the Son and keep him from the light of God's love. We can be influences for evil rather than good; we can become stumbling blocks to one another.

On the vine, if one branch is incorrectly pruned and infection enters, that infection can spread to the whole plant. In our Christian fellowship, if one person yields to the false vinedresser's mistaken teaching, it has repercussions throughout the Christian community. Heresies set back the cause of Christ as they divide individuals and groups. The whole Christian world suffers when a well-known Christian is involved in a scandal. "No man is an island" is especially true within the Body of Christ.

One question that arises within the family of Christ is how we can help someone get back on course if he has succumbed to other pressures and is no longer abiding in the Vine.

Pious phrases and judgmental attitudes won't do it. Nor will preaching at the "out-of-focus" person about how he should not be disobedient. Louie and I are fortunate to have covenant brothers and sisters who, though they never "preach at us," nevertheless keep us accountable when we yield to pressures and become disobedient in the overuse of our time. Since Louie's bout with hepatitis they have taken this responsibility much more seriously, helping us to keep the kind of schedule and life style that enables us to abide. After being checked this way, I often find myself singing the hymn that ends with "let our ordered lives confess the beauty of Thy peace."

How many times our children have been used by the Lord to call us on something—criticism that would be

tough to take except for their tender, "Hey, Mom, I understand. Know why? Because I'm so much like you."

Identification, when honest, is a warm, affirming way
of demonstrating that truth can be spoken in love.

In our desire to correct others, it is also important to
remember that Jesus did not tell us to change people but
to love them. Many of us have what psychology calls the
"rescue fantasy." We try to rearrange people's lives and
provide them with a happy ending. That is clearly not
our job.

However, branches do need to support one another in
love. How well I remember the night when one of our
covenant brothers had "come clean" regarding his involvement in Watergate and was sentenced to prison. A group
of us met for an agape supper where we laughed and shed
some tears; mainly we were there to pray for and support
our brother and his family. We wanted very much to be
branches who were taking away some of the harshness
of that day, for natural branches protect one another from
the stormy weather by huddling together.

Of course, protecting can go too far, preventing us from
growing strong and being able to endure. But the gentle
interplay of branches, diffusing the harshness of the sun
or the trauma of wind, without interfering with long-range
strengthening, can be a beautiful and redeeming thing.
Friends who join with us to laugh and pray alleviate the
harshness of the situation by their presence in our pain
when we're under pressure.

It is only as each branch abides in Jesus, the Vine, that
it can help other branches. This is true because it is the
energy of the Vine ministering to the branch in and
through other branches. The only way I can be helpful,
ministering blessing to other branches, is by abiding
closely in Jesus myself. *His* energy works within me to
accomplish this and the resulting fruit glorifies the Father.

Our love for our fellow branches—particularly tender,

new branches—needs to be coupled with God's wisdom. And God has proclaimed a dormant period for all tender shoots to allow quiet inner growth.

Throughout the plant kingdom, the time required for the dormant period varies greatly from one species to the next. One may require a few weeks, another months, others a whole winter or even several years. This variation applies to Christians, too. Few of us have the same rate of growth. Some young Christians are ready to shoulder a major responsibility sooner than others. We are all unique and answer to our Lord directly, not to any man-made formula.

It is important not to press new Christians into trying to bear fruit too soon. God has a perfect timetable for each one of us in this respect. Yet the human tendency is to exploit new Christians, particularly if they are leaders in the community or persons in public life. Yet we are told in the Apostle John's first epistle that we are not to be "respecters of persons."

I saw this abuse—and grieved over it—in Hollywood when well-known actors and actresses had genuine encounters with the living Lord. Seldom were they given opportunity to grow in faith before they were thrust onto the stage to give their testimony.

In Washington, D.C., it happens to public figures of a different sort. Being pressured into a "Christian celebrity" mold can disillusion the new convert about his fellow Christians and set him back spiritually before he's walked more than a few steps down the road of his new life.

A new branch cannot bear fruit until it is strong enough to bear its weight. If given too much weight to carry, it breaks.

A vivacious author shared with me recently some of her problems when she was pushed by well-meaning Christians to do too much too soon. She had to battle for time to be at home where she found the nourishing quiet to strengthen her spirit. To gain this quality time, she has suffered misunderstanding, and even hostility from "good Christian people" who fail to honor her needs when she disappoints their plans.

Not only are new Christians exploited by being honored for who they are rather than for Whom they serve, but it happens to mature Christians in ministry as well. Often they are given no opportunity to rest between meetings, conferences and nonstop speaking trips. Hounded by well-intentioned seekers who are eager for every morsel, these gifted people—especially the "well known"—can become depleted under grueling schedules that leave no time for breathing and abiding.

To be fair, we have to say that the ultimate responsibility for correcting the calendars of exploited people—whether they are tender new branches in the Vine or sturdy old-timers—belongs to the exploited. For men and women in ministry, the temptation to try and be all things in all places is heady wine. Yet greater sensitivity could clearly be exercised by those of us who extend the invitations even though we can't possibly know all the pressures a person may be enduring. And it is alarming how secular we Christians can act with Christian celebrities—embarrassingly eager to list their worldly accomplishments, to praise them rather than their Maker.

Young fruit must be allowed to ripen and develop slowly to maturity. If we want the ultimate flavor of the grape, we must not let the birds steal the fruit before it is ready to be harvested. The fruit needs time to fit into the unique plan God has for it. When this happens fruit is born that has richness of texture and is a delight to the Lord.

If the world hates you, know that
it has hated Me before it hated you
. . . If they persecuted Me, they will
persecute you . . .

Crushed Grapes

These verses on hatred and persecution give me a jolt. We who abide are called to joy, love, friendship, partnership with God, yes—but we are also called to suffer persecution. If good wine is to be produced, the fruit must be sacrificed, the grapes crushed.

Why have Christians so often been hated? The Roman government hated them because it viewed them as disloyal citizens. Caesar-worship was the unifying factor in the Roman Empire, and since Christians clearly did not conform they were a threat to the empire. If only they would say, "Caesar is Lord!"—even with tongue in cheek. But the Christians refused. Jesus alone was Lord. They would in no way concede; they would not play the game of paying homage to Caesar, and they were therefore considered dangerous. Persecution came because they put Christ first. Persecution will come to a person who dares to do that— even today.

113

First-century Christians were often accused of cannibalism. This charge came from a misunderstanding of the words of the sacrament: "This is My body which is for you . . . This cup is the new covenant in My blood . . . eat . . . drink" (1 Corinthians 11:24–26). There were vicious rumors about how the table of our Lord was prepared.

Further, Christians were said to be immoral and promiscuous because of their love feasts and the kiss of peace Christians gave one to another in greeting. These things were naturally misunderstood by those looking for something to misunderstand. A holy sign of Christian love was twisted by a few into rumors of sexual indulgence.

Christians were also hated because it was said that they "tampered with family relationships"—that families were divided because of their beliefs. There was some truth to this charge. Christ brings peace, yes, to the believer. But sometimes, to believe in Jesus brings not peace but a sword. When a wife becomes a Christian and a husband does not—when children or young people have a life-changing experience, but their parents do not—there is division. This sword came between people then, and it can do so today.

Most people are suspicious of those who are different. The person who radically follows Jesus is different. It is not easy to have the courage to stand up and be counted as Christians when we know ahead of time we will be judged unkindly. The world is not comfortable with goodness; it can even be dangerous to be good. Nonconformity is suspect. The world—that is, society without God— would be more comfortable with everybody fitting into its mold. But as followers of Christ we are told not to fit into the world's mold but to submit ourselves to be made like Him. Being different is difficult—risky—and yet the Kingdom demands that we take that risk. If we are not different people, we are probably not abiding in union with Jesus.

Recently a group in our congregation has been wrestling

with the concept of simpler life styles—that is, seeking ways to simplify our lives so that our discipleship will be more credible. It is sobering to see how much we are controlled by our society and how easy we are influenced by the values of our peers rather than the teachings of our Lord. When we do begin to change the way we live in some practical way, we often meet with resistance from those around us.

I was interested in reading about a man heading one of the nation's large businesses who switched from driving a large expensive limousine to a small compact car so that more of his wealth could be shared with others. This discomforted some of his peers, and they chided him for it. Our family has occasionally known that sort of pressure too. We drive a small, well-worn economy car. The last car we drove went 240,000 miles before it literally had to be towed to wherever old, broken-down cars go. There have been times when we've been chided, too, for this. And although this kind of resistance is a long way from suffering persecution, it is the kind of subtle pressure many of us will experience as we move into different life styles, seeking to abide in Christ and allow Him to reshape our lives in simple, practical, everyday ways. We find it easy to simplify through keeping our old cars running because we have so many good mechanics in our family, but in other ways we fall far short in our efforts. We are mere beginners, still very much "in process" when it comes to learning to simplify and thereby live compassionately for others.

In ways both large and small the person who abides in Christ, the Crucified One, will know what it means to be crucified with Him. Jesus, the highest example we have as Christians, approaches us not with a model of popular acclaim by the world but with the promise of persecution. "If any man would come after Me, let him deny himself and take up his cross and follow Me" (Mark 8:34).

Paul did it. Innocent, yet jailed, he used the time of imprisonment and persecution to reach his jailer with the

message of Jesus. But we don't have to go back to biblical
days for examples of people suffering for their faith.

Before the fall of Idi Amin's regime we received a letter
from Bishop Festo Kivengere, telling of the suffering and
persecution his people in Uganda had been undergoing
for their faith. He wrote with emotion, asking Christian
friends for "help to meet the desperate physical, spiritual,
and social needs of Uganda's tragedy-scarred refugees."

We have other family friends who have been ministering
in North Africa for years. Recently we learned that the
husband and father of the family was killed by crossfire—
the cost he and his family paid for the privilege of being
ambassadors for Christ in the country they loved and
served.

Dietrich Bonhoeffer knew something of this kind of suffering for Christ when he said, "When Christ calls a man,
He bids him come and die. It may be a death like that
of the first disciples, or like that of Luther leaving a monas-
tery." Bonhoeffer's point—that discipleship involves leaving a former way of life behind—is that death may come
to any part of our lives that separates us from God and
others.

"So shall your times of affliction become your times of
choicest blessing," Andrew Murray wrote. He felt affliction was "preparation for fruitfulness" and led into "closer
fellowship with the Son of God, and deeper experience
of His love and grace."

A recent article on persecution in *Christianity Today*
pointed out that while we modern Christians have a tendency to reject suffering, the early Christians embraced it,
knowing that Jesus learned obedience through what He
suffered. Paul, the great, teaching Apostle, chose to share
the sufferings of Christ. Christian martyrs from centuries
past are still models for the believers who are being persecuted for their faith in many countries around the world
today.

But what about here in the U.S.—the arena in which

most of us live out our faith? Certainly—and gratefully—
we are not persecuted for *believing* in Christ. The first
amendment of the Constitution takes care of that. But what
about the more subtle persecution that comes as a result
of applying what we believe to our everyday lives—the
translation of our creeds into deeds? Perhaps this is where
we in the United States will most often be called to "take
up our cross" and follow Him.

Very early in my life as a Christian I remember hearing
Dr. Louis Evans, Sr., who was my pastor at the time, teach
on the dual theme of the joy of knowing Christ and the
very real cost of following Him. These were never separate
themes in his preaching but as he put it, "two beats of
the same great heart." In one sermon he spoke of the early
Christians being driven by the Romans onto icefloes, there
to freeze—and then he added his warning that to live the
faith today could mean to be "driven out of society to
freeze in isolation."

From another message I remember: "Yesterday's believers were beaten with rods; today they may be scourged
with scorn or lashed by laughter."

And how often he reminded us of Christ's promise: "If
they persecute Me, they will persecute you." Then he
would add, "If Christ's promise is true, we shall be judged
not only by our successes but by our scars."

Soon after I became a member of Hollywood Presbyterian Church I well remember his preaching against a social
problem within the community. His sermons were powerful and far reaching, as they were broadcast every Sunday
night on prime time. Soon they began to have a strong
influence on public opinion. Then, as a result of his stand,
the economy of a powerful industry was threatened, and
a concerned friend within the police community warned
him that his life was in danger. Rather than heeding the
warning, he redoubled his efforts! His friend came to him
again and urged him to carry a clearly visible revolver
for his protection as he walked from his garage to his

house. This friend added, "If you will let me know when you'll be coming and going, I can assure you that other protective eyes will be watching." He gently declined the offer.

Dr. Evan's perseverance in what he clearly saw as a struggle for right was to him an inherent part of his faith. Observing him impressed upon me the truth that Christ not only lavishes love and joy and new life on His followers but that hand in hand come costly challenges and, at times, suffering and persecution.

Although Louie and I have never had to rely on "protective eyes"—other than the Lord's—we have received hate letters, obscene phone calls and a good many icy stares when we felt compelled to take unpopular stands in order to be true to our beliefs or to be involved in seeking justice.

The beatitudes have always spoken to me most clearly about the way Jesus wants us to live. As I ponder them and apply them to my own life I am amazed again at what following Christ may cost.

If we are humble (poor in spirit) the proud and arrogant may call us foolish.

If we are tamed and trained by God (meek) those who are self-made may call us weak.

If we are transparently honest (pure) we may irritate those who feel uncomfortable with the truth.

If we are generous (merciful) we may be known as a soft touch.

If we believe God's ways are best (seek goodness) we may be called prudes.

If we are peacemakers we may be called weaklings—even traitors—by those who want war.

Yes, *if* we live God's way, the suffering which Jesus promised will be part of the fabric of our lives.

Suffering should be considered a promise for all who abide in the Vine. The beautiful fruit must be sacrificed for even ordinary wine to be produced. Unless the skin is burst and the pulp cells crushed to release their juices the grape cannot become sacramental wine. The grape exists for purposes beyond its own self-interest and identity. Sacrifice and loss of selfhood, ironically, are its ultimate goal.

I read in a news magazine recently that the greatest wine has always been made where the vine is at its extreme climatically, when the grape is right on the edge of its endurance. To produce the finest wine, the vine must struggle for survival: an overabundance of water and nutrients make the resulting wine uninteresting and flat. By thrusting its roots deep into the soil the plant provides for the roots a constant environment—thus making possible the highest quality grapes. The roots of some vines reach a depth of 30 to 40 feet! In the same way, the struggling Christian who submits to the Vine is strengthened as difficulties are overcome, testing is met—the "hard road" roots going down deep into the soil of God's marvelous love.

Among many Christians today, however, we have a shallow understanding of suffering. When struggle or persecution come, we are apt to hear or even to say, "Why me? It's not fair. What did I do wrong?" Actually it might well mean that something very *right* was done for God.

For 30 years there have been reports of persecution of Christians in China following the Communist takeover in the late 1940s, such as Bibles being burned in the streets by officials; in Shanghai YMCA workers being forced to kneel by the Bibles as they burned until their cheeks and hands were blistered from the fire; over the years church buildings in China being pillaged, closed down or turned into warehouses; Chinese Christians being tortured or killed if they did not repudiate their beliefs.

Did this persecution wipe out the pockets of Christians throughout this immense land? Not at all. In fact, recent reports coming out of the new China, with its more open and friendly attitude toward the United States, indicate the opposite. In a *Time* magazine article, titled "The

Church That Would Not Die," I read how the church
went underground and grew. Groups of three and four
began meeting in homes. Soon the numbers grew to 30,
then to 50. They would sing, pray, study Bible passages
carefully copied by hand and listen to a message from
one of their own. Persecution helped create thousands of
small, self-contained Christian communities which have
operated in secret, mostly without ordained ministers—
often, even without Bibles.

And so it is for abiding Christians whose lives are laid
down for others just as Jesus' life was laid down for us.
We are called to share His suffering—not suffering for
the sake of suffering, but for the redemption of mankind:
for God and His right causes. While not pretending to
be parallel in suffering, we identify with biblical characters
and saints through the ages who have endured pain for
the faith. Karl Barth wrote, "Except we see the cross of
Golgotha, we cannot hear the gospel at the crib of Bethle-
hem."

The history of Christianity reveals that where it's easy
to be a Christian, so-called Christians are likely to be abundant—also insipid, weak and uninteresting, knowing little
of the strength that comes from abiding in Jesus the Vine.
But let persecution come—let Christianity become ille-
gal—and the handful of believers can change the course
of nations!

But even these courageous examples, when seen next
to the great example of our Lord, are faded and pale. His
suffering and persecution on our behalf are beyond com-
parison. Yet we benefit from it eternally, and in some
small way, participate in it right here on earth.

Persecution? Yes, it's promised. At some point we will
be like crushed grapes. But there is more: "Blessed are
those who are persecuted for righteousness' sake, for theirs
is the kingdom of Heaven. Blessed are you when men
revile you and persecute you and utter all kinds of evil
against you falsely on my account. Rejoice and be glad,

for your reward is great in heaven, for so men persecuted
the prophets who were before you. You are the salt of
the earth . . . You are the light of the world . . . Let
your light so shine before men, that they may see your
good works [the fruit of your abiding in Jesus the Vine]
and give glory to your Father who is in heaven" (Matthew
5:10–16).

The Life Sap

Recently I was sitting at the water's edge of a lake we love in the High Sierra. I pondered the great and mysterious work of the Counselor in the life of the believer. He is the Comforter, the Helper, the Holy Spirit, and He provides the life-giving sap—the very essence of spiritual strength—for us Christians. Louie and the boys were up the hill a short distance from me. I could hear them pounding nails into the dock we were building as a family project. They were laughing, teasing, yelling at each other. I savored those happy noises.

Just a rock and a tree away lay two rubber rafts. One was buoyant, filled with air and wonderfully functional, taking us one at a time to distant coves, supporting us as we floated by the hour, beautifully fulfilling its destiny and purpose. The other lay deflated, unused. Its compressed gas cylinders were unreleased; it was unable to keep even itself afloat, much less be of service to anyone.

How often we Christians are like that deflated raft, I thought. Because we are not filled with the Spirit we are flat, unbuoyant, unable to serve others or reach our own God-given destiny. To remedy this we are told: "Ask your Father for the Spirit . . . and He will give it" (Luke 11:9–13).

Jesus is telling us here that we can trust God to give us good gifts—that He longs for us to ask, to seek, to knock so that we can receive and find and have doors opened to us. He assures us that if we ask for the Holy Spirit, that is exactly what we will receive, because our Father in Heaven longs to give us only gifts that are good.

The plan is so beautiful, so simple. *But why,* I wondered, *are we so often reluctant to ask for more of Him in our lives? How sad and self-defeating to try to live for Christ, to bear fruit for Him and not know where to find the power and help we will need.*

Are we fearful that to be full of His essential, life-giving sap would make us religious freaks? True, we will be considered different—we will *be* different. But isn't that part of the cost, part of not being ashamed of the gospel? Being different is an inherent part of our walk in the Spirit with Christ. We *are* called to be a set-apart, "peculiar" people.

Have we feared that yielding to the Spirit would do violence to our personalities? But surely if we have been created by God for certain purposes, there has been planted within us already a deep desire to fulfill these purposes, a desire which the Spirit would only liberate and make fruitful. As one of my old friends put it as she began to experience the work of the Spirit in her life: "I feel as though I'm discovering the very *me* of *me!*"

The Holy Spirit would not do something out of keeping with God's design. We can trust the Father, the Son and the Holy Spirit completely, knowing that the Giver always makes sure our gifts are matched to the persons we were created to be.

Paul tells us that the Spirit comes that we may be "filled

with all the fullness of God" (Ephesians 3:19). The Greek word for fullness means *overflowing*. Not half full or even full-full, but I can be full to overflowing—splashing over from within my life!

How can I have that? By asking, we are told. By letting go of all that could hinder my relationship with God. By giving up an undue preoccupation with myself so that the God-created "me of me" might blossom and bring forth heavenly fruit.

As I watched Louie and the boys hike down the hill to the lake, a prayer formed in my mind:

"Jesus, I want all of You my life can hold—even to overflowing. Take from me the things that are standing in the way and fill me up with Yourself. I want to abide with You, stay close to You and bear beautiful fruit for Your glory."

How does this life-giving sap begin to flow through the branches? Not always in the same way, I've discovered. Some months ago my good friend, Jeanine Arnold, and I were sitting at the kitchen table in her Capitol Hill townhouse. A welcoming fire crackled in the fireplace, and steamy mugs of coffee perched in front of us. I felt good and warm inside, with a deep gratitude for friends like Jeanine. Suddenly I realized there was much I did not know about her spiritual journey.

When I asked about it, Jeanine shared easily how she became a Christian at 13, then sank into a kind of spiritual limbo, not growing in her faith. She had said to God in effect, "Now, Lord, You can come so far and no further. I want You in my life, I believe in You, but there are certain things that I'd rather take care of myself."

As Jeanine refilled our cups she continued, "I was afraid of what God might want from me if I totally surrendered to Him—afraid that He might send me off to the mission field or not let me live the kind of life I wanted. And so I led a double life—outwardly a Christian but inwardly uncomfortable around people who were really enthusiastic about Jesus. In fact, I was a bit ashamed of the gospel of Christ except at church and in the privacy of my own prayer life."

"Something must have happened along the way," I interjected, finding it difficult to imagine my radiant friend ever being complacent about the Lord.

Jeanine nodded. "I muddled along for years before the Lord brought me, step by step, to the point where I was willing to let Him enter every area of my life. Then I prayed that God would fill me with His Spirit. I wanted— at times, I demanded—an *experience*, something miraculous and overwhelming. But it never happened. Instead, God led me quietly closer to Himself, slowly revealing to me the areas of my life where I still wanted to be in charge. As I surrendered gradually, He filled me gradually without my being consciously aware of it.

"Finally I reached the point where I acknowledged— and accepted—the presence of the Spirit in my life. And that's how He continues to work in me. Nothing dramatic; but there is a sharp difference in my life now as compared to 10 or even five years ago."

"Can you define the difference?" I asked.

"I have much more awareness of God's love for all kinds of people. As I walk through the city, I find myself speaking to people I would have tried to avoid eye contact with before. I have an undercurrent of joy even in times of unhappiness—a knowledge that God is with me and will help. There is more inner peace as I learn to turn more of my worries over to God—not an easy thing for me, especially in practical matters like money."

Jeanine's eyes clouded slightly. "There are times I have *less* peace—or certainly less complacency—when I consider my responsibilities in Washington. How can I best serve Christ in this city that has so many needs?"

As we cleared away the coffee cups, we both agreed that although we are not always "comfortable" as the Spirit works in our lives, we would not exchange the excitement of this growing, abiding relationship with Christ for anything else in the world.

The quiet way the Holy Spirit is working in Jeanine's life is uniquely right for her. Yet I've observed that God meets each of us in the way that we individually need to be met. There's no specific way or time that He fills people with His Spirit. Today, just as in the early church, it can vary from person to person, from place to place. For some, it comes with the laying on of hands, as with the Ephesian Christians (Acts 19:6). With others, the Holy Spirit falls down upon them sovereignly as with the believers gathered in the upper room at Pentecost (Acts 2:2–4) and in the household of Cornelius (Acts 10:44–48). God always moves in His time and in His way (John 3:8).

Paul states: ". . . be filled with the Spirit" (Ephesians 5:18). The Greek translation for "filled" indicates a continuing present tense and more truly means "be filled again and again and again." So it was with Peter. At Pentecost he was one of those filled with the Spirit and preached a stirring sermon leading to the conversion of "about three thousand souls" (Acts 2:41). Yet days, maybe weeks later, Peter was again "filled with the Spirit" as he spoke with great power to the Jewish rulers and elders (Acts 4:8). Still later, when Peter and John returned to their companions (believers whom we assume experienced the Pentecost filling), they were all *again* "filled with the Spirit" (Acts 4:23, 31).

And so it has been for me. I felt the blessing of the Spirit's presence in my own life when I first surrendered to Christ. Since that time I've had other experiences with the Holy Spirit—second, third and fourth blessings, I've called them. Though I clearly felt His initial coming into my life when I said yes to Jesus, the process of discovering specific gifts of the Spirit in operation is a continuing journey.

I must admit there are some days when I feel the Spirit

more than I do on other days, but from the beginning there's been no doubt that He has been there always. I know that not so much by my feelings but because Jesus himself promised that His Spirit would never leave me (John 14:16).

Christ has made His presence felt in me in many ways. First, I was filled with a love that had a different quality about it, like nothing I had ever experienced before. It wasn't more of something I had already had—it was something new, from a different source. Then there was joy— not happiness or something giddy but something deep and warm inside.

Like Jeanine, sometimes, I find the Spirit makes me feel restless—uneasy, convicted about some situation, uncomfortable until I have taken some difficult step or made a needed change in my life. Sometimes He nudges me so hard with a spiritual "poke in the ribs" that I am led to do something that would never have entered my mind without His direct guidance. At other times, He keeps me company with His comforting presence when my heart is aching and only His healing touch can reach the pain. But always the work of the Spirit is practical, dealing with everyday life.

Some people who have grown up as believers don't recall ever having an experience with God. As with Jeanine, some may have gone through a gradual yielding to the Holy Spirit, a growing awareness of His presence in them. Louie was also a believer for as long as he could remember, but nonetheless he was overwhelmed by the rush of the Holy Spirit into his life the moment he yielded in confession and submitted his whole being to Christ. "Being filled with the Holy Spirit the first time was, for me, like being hit by a 20-ton truck," he says.

Not infrequently, this special experience with the Holy Spirit is preceded by what many refer to as the worst period in their lives. When pressures and tensions mount beyond bearing, when they learn that they are not able to handle life without help, they are brought to their knees in some unexpected way. Onlookers are quick to recognize that the "Hound of Heaven" may have been pursuing such a person, lovingly trying to persuade him to surrender totally to God.

Josh was another believer who for years had a one-dimensional faith. A good organizer and doer, he was given job after job in his church because of his ability to get things done.

One day he rebelled. It happened when he felt pressured to take on still another responsibility at a church meeting. At the close of the meeting Josh erupted, accused the committee chairman of having forced him to sign up for the activity. The chairman promptly removed Josh's name from the list, and Josh stormed home in a fury.

Embarrassed and upset by her husband, Josh's wife questioned his behavior. Angrily he snapped back at her, "I have never been more surrounded by loving Christian friends. Nor have I ever studied God's Word more diligently. And yet, with all this, I am more miserable than I have ever been in my entire life. If this is Christianity, I don't want any part of it. Furthermore, I don't care if I *ever* do another thing for the church!"

Aware that a crucial spiritual battle was going on inside himself, Josh asked a fellow Christian to come to his home and help him pray it through. As the friend prayed for Josh to know the fullness of the Spirit, a gradual calm and peace descended over him, a sense of deep comfort, and a knowledge that God was, in fact, in his life. He started praising God, silently at first, and then to his surprise out loud in unknown yet meaningful syllables.

Listening to the new words cascading so effortlessly from his lips, Josh rejoiced as he realized that the Holy Spirit had taken over inside him and was praying to the Father about every aspect of his jammed-up life. Frustration, reluctance, resentment, anger, self-centeredness— they all fell away like broken fetters as the prayer continued. As the syllables flowed forth, Josh would exclaim inwardly, *Oh, yes, Lord, don't forget that!*

For Josh, the experience with the Holy Spirit was so intense and Jesus was made so real to him that he spent over an hour on his knees. "I didn't want to stop praying until the Spirit had prayed about everything in my life and I had turned it all over to God," he said.

Josh's personality was not changed by this experience, but there is a qualitative difference in his life—a new strength and underlying joy, a diminishing reaction to his former frustrations. His attitude is different; he has become more tolerant. Now he is able to listen for what God wants him to do, not just for what people want. He can say "yes" to God and a loving "no" to people without feeling guilty or pressured.

Both Louie and I have had strong—sometimes painful—experiences in which the Lord has had to show us how needy we are. One such time for me was the sudden death of my mother. A different but unforgettable experience happened in Louie's life several years ago.

Our two older boys had been attending college in the West and were going to meet the rest of us for vacation at Bass Lake, our starting place for backpacking into the High Sierra. Jamie and Andie were still in high school and were driving with us from our home in Washington, D.C., to California. On the first day of our trip, Louie was talking about how tired he had been, of how much there was to do and how little time to get it all done.

Our spiritually sensitive Andie had been listening carefully, resting her chin on the back of the driver's seat. "Your problem is that you run so fast all the time, Daddy. You just don't take enough time to sit down with the Lord. No wonder you get so tired. I think you should get away all by yourself on this trip and just be with God."

We all agreed with this wisdom, and Louie decided he would do this toward the end of our vacation. Then we gathered together, the six of us, as we've done many times

in the past 20 years and drove up to a little rented cabin
on the shore of Bass Lake.

Several days later we drove an hour further up the un-
paved lumber road, parked our car, donned packs and made
our way through the gentle wilderness where we set up
camp on the shore of a high, snow-fed lake. The setting
was indescribably beautiful—gigantic panoramas—filling
us with an awe of the God who created it all.

After about a week of sharing the splendor, the kids
and I packed up and headed for the cabin down the mountain, leaving Louie alone for his time with the Lord. To
my surprise, I had a real struggle with leaving him. My
eyes kept puddling up and the kids began giving me a
bad time about it.

"Come on, Mom. You'll see Dad again in four days.
It's not good-by forever."

I knew they were right. I knew, too, that Louie needed
the time alone. Still I was uneasy.

Two nights later, soon after I fell asleep in the safety
and relative comfort of our little cabin down the big mountain, I awakened abruptly. I looked at the clock on the
bedstand: it was 2 A.M. Louie was heavy on my mind! I
was aware that he had some need, but I didn't know what
it was or what I could do about it except to pray, "Lord,
take care of him up there." I had to trust my husband to
God's keeping. My "holy restlessness" continued through
the night. Over and over again I had to remind myself,
"Have no anxiety about anything, but in everything by
prayer and supplication with thanksgiving . . ." (Philippians 4:6–7). I'd doze awhile, then wake up to pray again.

When dawn finally came, I rolled out of bed—and found
Tim already in the kitchen. "Tim, it's a big thing to ask—
but would you mind terribly hiking back up the mountain
to check on your dad? I've been uneasy about him all
night . . ."

On the second of his "solo" days, Louie had climbed
to another tiny lake near a lush meadow at 11,000 feet

where he had spent hours in study, prayer and quiet meditation. "It was fantastically beautiful there," he told us later. "The kind of day that makes you ultra-sensitive to all the beauty around you, vibrantly aware of the living presence of God. The Holy Spirit just kept dropping ideas into my mind." The ideas had come so rapidly that he had completed a year's preaching outline in just one day!

After this productive time, Louie had felt a prodding in his consciousness: *Get back to camp.* Obedient to the nudge, he had packed his papers and books into his backpack, assembled his fishing gear and started to hike down. Coming to a clear lake, he could see trout jumping in the early evening shadows, inviting him to stop for a catch.

He fished for a while, but again the urging came more insistent than before: *Get back to camp.* Reluctantly he packed up his fishing equipment and headed down the mountainside. Just minutes from his camp a sudden and excruciating pain struck in his right lower back. It was so intense he staggered the remaining distance to camp. *Is it my heart?* he thought. *Perhaps a kidney stone?* He took a long drink from his canteen of water, then trembling with pain, he stumbled toward the tent as waves of weakness swept over him. The pain was so agonizing he was soaked with perspiration.

Somehow he crawled into the tent and climbed into his sleeping bag. He tried to take his pulse, fighting off panic. He could tell his pulse was growing weaker and weaker. Then he began to pray.

"I was helpless and immobilized," he said later. "There was just God and myself. I called for His help. Then I began to sing a familiar hymn: 'Come Holy Spirit, Heavenly Dove, with all Thy healing power . . .'

"Then out of the deep past came the words, 'Jesus loves me this I know, for the Bible tells me so . . .' I was surprised at the fervor of these words. Tears ran down my face as the words flowed out. 'Oh, how I love Jesus . . . oh, how I love Jesus . . .'

"Then I found myself repeating verses of the 19th Psalm I had been memorizing that day, verses that spoke of the heavens declaring the glory of God . . . 'day unto day uttereth speech, and night unto night sheweth knowledge . . .' The feverishness of my initial panic began to ebb as the verses edged back into my consciousness: 'The fear of the Lord is clean, enduring for ever: the judgments of the Lord are true and righteous altogether . . . Let the words of my mouth, and the meditation of my heart, be acceptable . . . O Lord my strength, and my redeemer.'

"For the first time in my life I spoke with syllables I did not understand with my mind, but my heart and spirit knew they were ecstatic utterances of praise. As the hours wore on, I continued to pray and ask God for his healing touch. I sang words and tunes I had never heard before. Then suddenly my body was racked with muscular convulsions in my midsection which were almost worse than the pain. I concentrated on relaxation and peace of mind. I sensed panic could be fatal.

"I looked at my watch: it was 2 A.M.; six hours since the pain began.

"At last the convulsions ceased. All was very quiet. I tried to find my pulse but could not. I felt hazy and distant. I tried to sing again, but my voice was only a low, gutteral rasp. *Is this the end?* I wondered. I seemed very close to the edge of a deep chasm. In those quiet moments I felt suspended in gentleness. I pictured that mountain valley, the orange tent and the man inside it cradled in the hand of God. Suddenly I knew this moment called for ultimate submission and trust. 'If You want me now, Lord, I am ready. But if I live, I am Yours afresh.' Then I was quiet— waiting—relaxed—and amazingly peaceful. I thanked God for Himself, for Colleen and the children, my covenant brothers and sisters and my two successors in the parishes I had served. Love and gratitude poured over me. 'I am thine, O Lord, I am thine.' "

As Louie lay there quietly waiting, he was aroused by a nibbling on his ear. Startled, he shook his head and heard the sound of tiny feet scampering nearby.

Hey, he thought, *if I'm going to die, that's all right. But Lord, not a rodent-eaten corpse!*

Louie found strength enough to make a loud "Psst!" sound, and a little chipmunk scampered out of the tent. With that his pulse quickened. Later he wondered if the little animal had been God's messenger.

"When I felt my pulse again," Louie said, "I took another big drink of water that emptied my canteen. Then about 6 A.M. the pain moved slowly across my back and was gone." By 7 A.M. he put together an emergency pack and started down the mountain on shaky legs.

Louie told us later that he felt stronger with each step, his eyes growing brighter at the full awareness of his encounter with God. At the bottom of the mountain he met Tim on his way up, who took one look at his father's drawn, ashen face and gasped, "Dad! What's happened?"

Louie embraced his strong, young son, looked into his eyes and said, "Tim, how did you know to come?"

His blue eyes intense with understanding, he said, "Mom thought you needed me."

To Louie, the experience had one inescapable conclusion: he was to live as a branch, totally dependent on Jesus the Vine. It was a relationship now solidly tested, vibrantly alive, strong as tempered steel.

Louie and I have both learned through this, more certain than ever before, that it is when we are at the end of ourselves that God's power is strongest in us. It was Hudson Taylor's concept of the "exchanged life." When we know we can't do anything, we let Him take over; we exchange our powerless life for His infinitely powerful one. Knowing we are completely dependent on Jesus the Vine for our courage, our strength, our love, our very breath, we make ourselves available to His Holy Spirit in that utterly dependent way that lets His power flow through us just as Christ means for it to flow *all* the time.

How sad that we so seldom tap into this power unless we're in a crisis. For his incredible strengthening power is available to us as a continual stream. We were never designed to be do-it-yourselfers even in the everyday routines of life. My search has come to an unalterable conclusion that our Christian lives are to be lived in such an abiding-in-Jesus-the-Vine way that the world cannot fail to see that it is *Christ in us,* by His life-giving sap, who is doing the living: Not I that live, but Christ who lives in me.

What would happen, I wondered, if we all recognized daily our utter dependence on the Lord as Josh did when he was brought to the end of himself, as Louie did when he was alone with God on the mountain, as I did the week my mother was taken from this earth? I think of John Alexander's words: "We can do nothing on our own and God intends for us to learn that." What would happen if we prayed each day from the depths of our hearts, "Lord, I want to be altogether Yours. I can do nothing without You. Live Your life through me today, Lord—really live through me. Let Your love, the love that the Father has for the Son, be in me today. Let Your obedience operate through me today."

What would happen if we so lived that we recognized our dependence on His power, not just in crisis situations—the power-in-a-pinch kind of thing—but in every single moment of our lives? What would happen if we always fit into His plan for how we are to live, abiding in Him, drawing all our needs from Him; not lifeless robots under His benevolent control, but very human, very real children of God, looking to Him, living in conscious union with Him, honoring and glorifying Him, bearing the fruit that is the inevitable result of abiding in Jesus our Vine?

What would happen?

Who can say?

But I want to find out by trying the experiment—going back to the basics and abiding in intimate union with Jesus the Vine, letting His Holy Spirit fill me and overflow from me to all those whose lives I touch for whatever purpose He wills and for the measure of time He grants me in this life.

How about you?